Reader's Digest

historic houses

Scotland

Hamish Scott

Contents

4 THE HIGHLANDS & ISLANDS

5 THE NORTHEAST

SHETLAND

Jarlshoff

ORKNEY

Kirbuster Farm · Broch of Gurness · Skara Brae · Skaill House · Corrigall Farm · Museum · Stromness · Kirkwall · Earl's Palace

Cairness House · Peterhead · Provost · Craigston Castle · Delgatie Castle · Fyvie Castle · Haddo House · Oldmeldrum · Castle Fraser

Duff House · Craigievar Castle · Corgarff · Ballindalloch Castle · Leith Hall · Huntly · Brodie Castle · Forres · Lossiemouth · Hugh Miller's Cottage · Cawdor Castle · Fort George · Fortrose · INVERNESS · Urquhart Castle · Dornoch · Dunrobin Castle · Stornoway · Arnol Blackhouse · Dun Carloway · Dunvegan Castle · Eilean Donan Castle · Castle of Mey

THE NORTHEAST

THE HIGHLANDS & ISLANDS

CENTRAL SCOTLAND 1

Montrose
The House of Dun
Arbroath
Edzell Castle 2
A90
A933
A932
Forfar
Glamis Castle 5
A926
A94
DUNDEE
St Andrews
Crail
Kellie Castle 13
Hill of Tarvit 8
A916
Elie
A923
Stobhall 6
Scone Palace 7
Newburgh
Kirkcaldy
Falkland Palace 9
A91
A92
Lochleven Castle
Perth
Kinross 12
M90
Dunfermline
North Berwick
Dunbar
Greywalls 8
Lennoxlove Hall 10
Dirleton Castle 1
Crichton Castle 12
Gosford House 7
Newhailes 11
Borthwick Castle 14
Inchcolm Abbey 2
Dalmeny House 6
EDINBURGH
Arniston House 13
A9
Blair Castle 1
Pitlochry
Castle Menzies 4
Crieff
A822
A924
CENTRAL SCOTLAND 1
Auchterarder
A823
Castle Campbell 11
Dollar
Culross Palace
Blackness Castle 3
House of the Binns 4
Linlithgow Palace 9
Alloa Tower 16
Falkirk
Callendar House 18
Bathgate
Doune Castle 10
Stirling
Argyll's Lodging
Stirling Castle 15
Airdrie
A803
GLASGOW & THE WEST 3
New Lanark 8
Lanark
M74
Tenement House 3
GLASGOW
Pollok House 4
Holmwood House 5
The Hill House 1
Helensburgh
Dumbarton
Newark Castle 2
Dean Castle 7
Kilmarnock
Cumnock
Dumfries House 10
Fort William
Inveraray Jail
Inveraray Castle 22 23
Largs
Kelburn Castle 6
Rothesay
Burns' Cottage 9
Ayr
Maybole
Culzean Castle 11
Blairquhan 12
Brodick Castle 25
Mount Stuart 24
Oban
Torosay Castle 20
Duart Castle 21
Lochgilphead
Campbeltown

The best in Britain

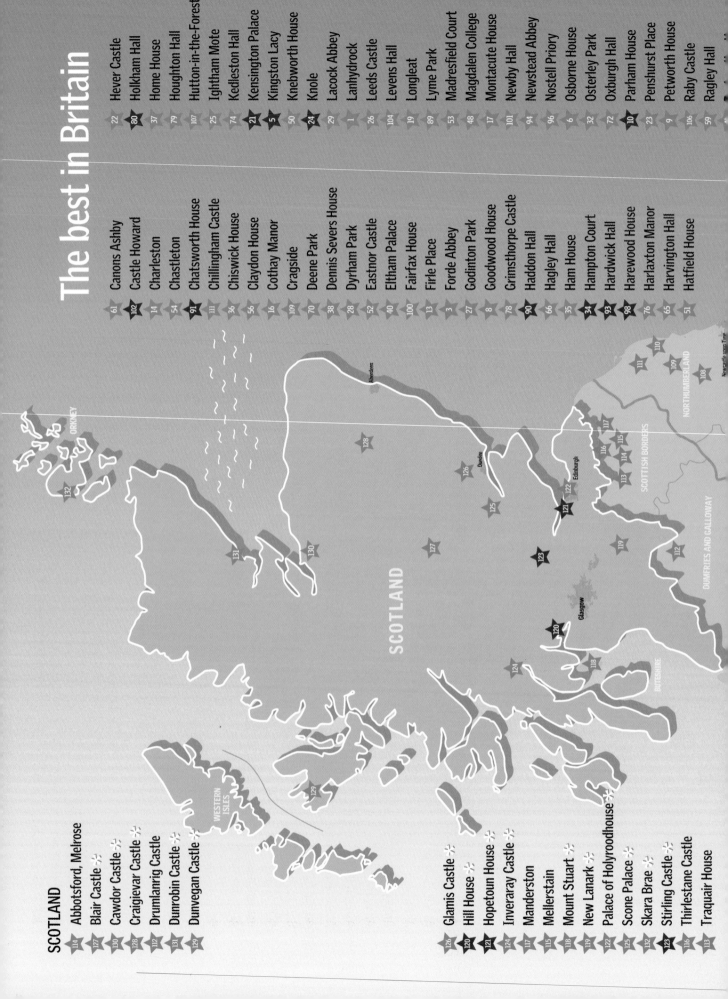

WALES

ENGLAND

Legend:
- 5 Star
- 4 Star
- ✶ Featured in this book

Scotland's houses deserve greater credit than they generally get from architectural historians. That, at least, is my conclusion after visiting almost every example open to the public and making a selection for this book. Castles dismissed as crude defensive structures turn out to be mansions reaching for the skies. The Baroque extravagances of the Restoration are a joy to behold. William Adam at his best was as brilliant as his sons, while Robert produced some of his best work in his final years back in Scotland. To top it all there is Charles Rennie Mackintosh. In writing of Scotland's splendours, and occasionally its oddities, I have been inspired by the wit and erudition of Simon Jenkins' masterly survey of houses in England, but the opinions here are entirely my own.

Hamish Scott

Historic houses
of Scotland

The Scotland covered here is a truncated version of the geographical entity, as the southernmost counties are with England's northernmost in the volume entitled **The Borders**.

Central Scotland, from Fife through to Stirling, including Perthshire and Tayside, straddles both a topographical and cultural frontier. Castles such as Blair and Doune command routes from lowland pastures into Highland glens while the royal stronghold at Stirling guarded a strategic river crossing between north and south. Other royal palaces include Falkland and Linlithgow, both largely 16th century. Scone Palace enjoys almost legendary status as a cradle of the nation's history. The misleadingly named Culross 'Palace' is a relatively modest merchants' house, beautifully restored by the National Trust for Scotland. A family's devotion to their adopted home ensured the survival of Kellie Castle, while a clan society was responsible for the renovation

of Castle Menzies. The Hill of Tarvit is an Edwardian evocation of the past.

As the hinterland of **Edinburgh, The Lothians** have always been home to prosperous and powerful families. The impressive ruins of Dirleton Castle evoke the splendours of a feudal household; Borthwick and Craigmillar were built as private strongholds in a later but still brutal age. In the capital itself, history can be traced from the medieval Castle, through the Renaissance Holyrood Palace and Old Town tenement of Gladstone's Land, to the classical sophistication of the Georgian House in the New Town. Of country houses in the Lothians, Newhailes saw the first tentative step towards Palladian formality, while Hopetoun witnessed the movement's triumph. Later in the 18th century, Robert Adam took architecture on another path with Gosford House.

Glasgow and the West, extending from Ayrshire to the Firth of Clyde, is proudly distinct from Scotland's 'softer' east, with a hard-edged history of migration, industry and trade. Of early tower houses Newark is an unusually original survival, Dean Castle has been thoroughly restored and Kelburn has grown old with an eccentric charm. Culzean, the greatest of the region's castles, is an aristocratic fantasy by Robert Adam in the late 18th century. The mills, tenements and schoolhouses of New Lanark reflect Robert Owen's vision of an industrious Utopia. Classical country houses are not well represented, other than by Dumfries House, which has just been saved for the nation. Alexander 'Greek' Thomson's Holmwood House is in a more experimental style. Mount Stuart on the Isle of Bute is a spectacular expression of *fin de siecle* Gothicism. It seems extraordinary that Charles Rennie Mackintosh's Hill House – one of the most iconic early modern buildings in Britain – was built just a few years later.

The Highlands and Islands are cut off by their mountains, yet lie open to the sea. In prehistoric times trading routes linked even the Northern Isles with distant lands and Skara Brae is the best of the early settlements offering a fascinating glimpse though time. Long after Scotland's birth, the region remained a place apart, with a Norse-Gaelic culture of its own. Strongholds of clan warlords, such as Dunvegan, line the wild west coast. Some, like Eilean Donan, are modern restorations, having been reduced to ruin during the half a century of Jacobite conflict that ended on Culloden Moor. Fort George was built to cow the rebellious population and is one of Britain's most impressive works of military engineering. In later years, the emptied glens became a playground for the rich and vast pleasure-palaces such as Dunrobin rose up. In recent times, a few examples of more humble dwellings have been carefully preserved. Some, such as Kirbuster on Orkney, are of almost prehistoric simplicity.

The Northeast, from Angus up to Moray, is a land of castles. Dunnottar is a soul-stirring sea-fortress, now in ruins, but it is the tower houses such as Craigievar and Crathes that truly fire the imagination. Built by several generations of master-masons by the name of Bel, these romantic, multi-storeyed mansions represent the high point of Scots Renaissance architecture. In utter contrast, and dating from the first half of the 18th century, there are classical masterpieces such as Duff House, Haddo and the House of Dun, all by William Adam. A century later, Queen Victoria's devotion to Balmoral made both the traditions and landscapes of the region fashionable, leading to the enlargement of old tower houses such as Fyvie and Ballindalloch.

☆ STAR RATINGS AND ACCESSIBILITY ☆☆☆☆☆

The 'star' ratings follow the system devised by Simon Jenkins, who reviewed all the houses in England and Wales that feature in *Discover Britain's Historic Houses*. In selecting those entries, Simon Jenkins defined the term 'house' as embracing 'any structure in which men and women have laid their heads, provided they are in some degree accessible to public view'.

The stars rate the overall quality of a house as presented to the public, and not gardens or other attractions, although in Scotland the setting of a house may be an intrinsic part of its appeal. On balance, houses are scaled down for not being easily accessible or only partly open. The top rating, five stars, is given to houses that qualify as 'international' celebrities. Four stars go to houses of outstanding historic significance, architectural quality and public display. Three-stars indicate good historic houses, well displayed and worthy of national promotion. Two and one-star houses are of more local interest, are hard to visit, or have just one feature.

Accessibility varies greatly, from buildings that are open all year to houses that can only be visited 'by appointment'. Opening hours tend to alter from year to year, but an indication of how accessible a house is to visitors is given at the start of each entry, together with brief information on location and ownership. Many of the houses are owned or run by the National Trust for Scotland or Historic Scotland, some are now museums or hotels, others are privately owned by families who open to the public for part of the year. More details are given at the back of this book, and readers are advised to check before visiting.

A final note, houses are, or should be, living things subject to constant change and how we view them is bound to be a subject of debate. We welcome any correction or comment, especially from house owners.

NOTE: On the UK map (pages 6-7) the 4 and 5-star houses in England and Wales were selected by Simon Jenkins. Those in Scotland were selected by Hamish Scott and the editors of Reader's Digest.

Architectural timeline
and Scotland's houses in brief

Aberdeen: Provost Skene's House
An important town house, built in 1545 but named after a 17th-century resident. Fine plasterwork and wall painting survive inside.

Alloa Tower
Tower of a 15th-century castle, most of which was demolished by the 6th Earl of Mar. A later building burnt down, leaving just the tower.

Arniston House
An 18th-century house around a medieval tower house. Begun by William Adam in 1726 and finished by his son, John.

Arnol Blackhouse
Sole survivor of a once-common type of home that changed little for a thousand years. Low rubble walls support a thatched roof.

Ballindalloch Castle
A 16-century, Z-plan tower, with wings added in the 1770s and 1850s. The interiors mix modern furnishings with historic pieces.

Balmoral
The Royal family's home in Scotland, built by Victoria and Albert in a suitably Scots Baronial style on the site of an earlier castle.

Blackness Castle
A 15th-century fortress, jutting into the Forth; extended in the 1540s it became the country's chief artillery fort and also served as a prison.

Blair Castle
Victorian castle, designed by David Bryce, around an 18th-century mansion, that in turn was built upon a medieval core. The interiors reflect the building's diverse history.

Blairquhan
A Regency mansion, designed in the 1820s by William Burn in English Tudor style. Inside, the saloon rises up through two floors with cantilevered galleries at the upper level.

Borthwick Castle
A 15th-century tower house, believed to be the tallest of its kind in Scotland.

Brodick Castle
Built on an earlier structure dating to the 13th century, Brodick was redesigned in the 19th as a grand Scots Baronial shooting lodge.

Brodie Castle
A Z-plan tower house dating from the mid-16th century and rebuilt after the Civil War with fine interiors and plasterwork.

Burn's Cottage
The thatched cottage in Alloway where Robbie Burns was born in January 1759. It was built by the poet's father in 1757.

Cairness House
A Georgian mansion, designed by James Playfair on neo-classical lines, incorporating contemporary architectural symbolism and Egyptian hieroglyphs.

Callendar House
A French-style mansion built in the 1860s around an earlier house, with medieval remains and a restored grand kitchen.

Castle Campbell
Ruined castle high above a gorge – built c1450 then extended in the early 1500s and early 1600s – with a partly restored tower.

Castle Fraser
A medieval castle, refashioned in the 1570s and again in the 1600s. The interiors were much altered in subsequent centuries.

Castle Menzies
A 16th-century Z-plan castle, with an 1840s wing by William Burn. The castle fell into ruin in the 1900s but has been restored.

Castle of Mey
Coastal castle a few miles from John O'Groats, built in the 1560s. It belonged to the late Queen Mother, and is preserved as she left it.

Cawdor Castle
A 14th-century castle built around a legendary 'Thorn Tree'. Fortified in the 1450s, extended in the 1600s, with Victorian additions.

Corgarff Castle
A remote castle dating from the mid-16th century. It became a military base in the 1740s, surrounded by a protective outer wall.

Craigievar Castle
A tall, 17th-century tower house, built by master-mason John Bel on an earlier structure, with distinctive battlements and turrets.

Craigston Castle
An early 17th-century castle, thought to be by master-mason John Bel, with an unusual façade topped by an arch and parapet.

Crathes Castle
Another of Bel's castles, from the late 16th century, built over an older building, with Renaissance painted ceilings.

Crichton Castle
A castle dating from a 1390s tower house, with three ranges added in the 1450s, plus an Italian inspired 16th-century range.

Culross Palace
A courtyard town house, built in the late 15th and early 16th centuries, by an early industrialist and wealthy merchant.

Culzean Castle
A romantic Georgian castle, designed by Robert Adam around a medieval tower, and still unfinished at the death of both Adam and his patron, the Earl of Cassillis.

Dalmeny House
A Regency mansion designed in Tudor style by William Wilkins, with architectural details made in pre-fabricated Coade stone.

Dean Castle
The keep dates from the late 14th century, the palace from the 15th, and the castle was heavily restored in the Edwardian era.

Delgatie Castle
A clan tower house dating from the 16th century, with claims to 11th-century origin, carefully restored in the 20th century.

STONE AGE · BRONZE AGE · IRON AGE · ROMAN BRITAIN · DARK AGES · EARLY MEDIEVAL

Kenneth MacAlpin r.c840-58 · Malcolm III r.1057-93 · David I r.1124-53 · Alexander III r.1249-86 · David III r.1329-71 · Robert the Bruce r.1306-29

2000BC 1000BC 0 500 800 1200 MEDIEVAL 1400

Dirleton Castle
The remains of a 12th-century castle with curtain wall and drum towers. Rebuilt into an impressive house in the 14th and 15th centuries, it was further added to in the 16th.

Doune Castle
A ruined medieval fortress sited on a river promontory and enclosed by a curtain wall.

Drum Castle
Medieval castle with a granite tower, extended with 16th and 17th-century wings and improved by David Byrne in the 19th century.

Duart Castle
Ancient island fortress, with a curtain wall built c1250 and keep c1390. It was added to in the 1670s and restored from ruins as the clan stronghold in 1911.

Duff House
Grand Baroque country house designed by William Adam, but beset by problems and still unfinished at Adam's death in 1748.

Dumfries House
One of Robert and John Adam's first grand houses, this Palladian mansion was built in the 1750s, with original furnishings including pieces by Chippendale.

Dun Carloway
A prehistoric broch, about 2000 years old, in a commanding spot overlooking a once-busy seaway. The stone tower is some 30 feet tall.

Dunnottar Castle
Atmospheric ruin on the site of a Pictish stronghold and early monastery. Earliest parts are 14th century but the remains of a 16th-century Renaissance palace can also be seen.

Dunrobin Castle
Palace built with the help of Sir Charles Barry, mixing Scots Baronial and French chateau. The interiors were restored by Robert Lorimer.

Dunvegan Castle
Macleod clan stronghold, with a massive keep added in the 14th century and Fairy Tower built c1500. It was rebuilt in the 1840s.

Edinburgh: Craigmillar Castle
A medieval castle, with early 15th-century tower house and additional buildings and ranges from the 16th and 17th centuries.

Brochs

There are some 700 brochs in Scotland, most of them in the northern tip of the country and in the Northern Isles. They date from the Iron Age, between 600BC and AD100, and are often positioned overlooking the sea. Their purpose is still uncertain: they may have been defensive structures, built to protect the local population from raiders, or they may have been constructed to impress, confirming the status of an important figure in the community.

Brochs are tall, circular towers, characterized by double-skinned dry-stone walls constructed without mortar. They consist of two concentric walls, joined at various points with stone lintel slabs, but otherwise hollow between the outer and inner walls. This double-walled technique produced a strong structure, allowing the broch builders to go higher than was possible with a single wall.

Most brochs were entered by a door at ground level. Inside was a central main chamber, from which smaller rooms led off, either within the hollow area between the two walls or simply butting up to the inner wall. Stone steps spiralled up between the inner and outer walls leading to upper floors, or perhaps just to a wooden gallery overlooking the main chamber.

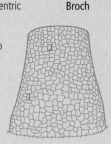
Broch

Edinburgh: Edinburgh Castle
Built on the site of several earlier fortresses, this medieval royal residence was transformed into a Renaissance palace in the 1490s. The subterranean prisons can still be seen.

Edinburgh: The Georgian House
7 Charlotte Square, designed by Robert Adam in 1791 as part of Edinburgh's New Town and preserved as a typical Georgian town house.

Edinburgh: Gladstone's Land
A six-storey tenement in Edinburgh's Old Town, completed in 1617 with a covered arcade and shop at ground floor level.

Edinburgh: Holyrood Palace
A late medieval palace built on the site of an Augustinian abbey founded by David I in 1128. Restored as a royal residence by Sir William Bruce for Charles II.

Edinburgh: John Knox House
Town house built in 1557, reputedly the home of John Knox in 1572. Owned by a goldsmith who would have used the ground floor.

Edinburgh: Lauriston Castle
A house refurbished in the early 20th century as the home of an Edwardian collector. The earliest part, a tower house, dates back to 1593; the house was rebuilt in 1825.

Edinburgh: Mary King's Close
The remains of a medieval street, once part of a network of narrow lanes that was built over in the 18th century. The buildings were not demolished, they were left beneath the city.

Edzell Castle
A ruined mansion, all that remains of a 16th-century house, now famed for its historic garden.

Eilean Donan Castle
A 20th-century castle built from the ruins of a medieval fortress on an island at the head of three sea lochs; the site has been of strategic significance since Pictish times.

Falkland Palace
A 15th-century hunting lodge, rebuilt in the 1530s by James V as a Renaissance-style palace and restored in the 1890s.

Fort George
A massive fortress with impressive defences built by George II after the defeat of Bonnie Prince Charlie at Culloden.

Fyvie Castle
A medieval courtyard house transformed in the late 16th century into a new castle showing French influence. Extended in the 18th century and modernized in the 19th.

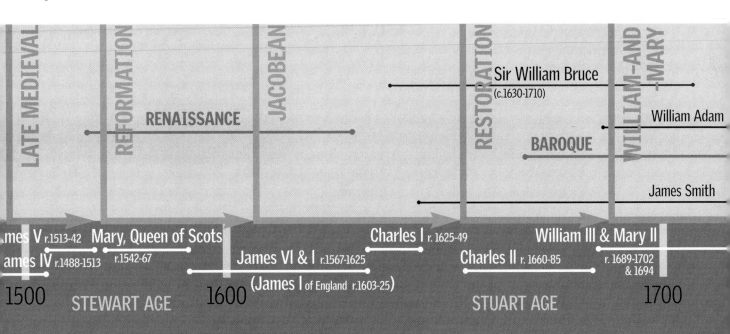

LATE MEDIEVAL

REFORMATION

RENAISSANCE

JACOBEAN

RESTORATION

Sir William Bruce (c.1630-1710)

WILLIAM-AND-MARY

William Adam

BAROQUE

James Smith

James V r.1513-42   Mary, Queen of Scots   r.1542-67

James IV r.1488-1513

James VI & I r.1567-1625

(James I of England r.1603-25)

Charles I r. 1625-49

Charles II r. 1660-85

William III & Mary II

r. 1689-1702 & 1694

1500   STEWART AGE   1600   STUART AGE   1700

William Adam (1689–1748)

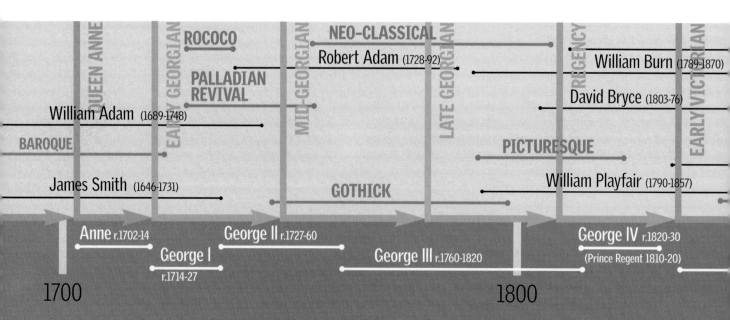

The man who became known as the 'Universal Architect of Scotland' began his career apprenticed to a mason before working for his father, a Kirkcaldy builder. He displayed an early flair for business, pursuing various schemes including coal mining, brewing and brick manufacture, and would turn his father's building firm into the largest in Scotland. Throughout his career he was as much a building contractor as an architect.

Adam's first grand designs were executed in the 1720s – the Edinburgh Royal Infirmary and Hopetoun House (page 75) being the most notable. In 1728 he became Clerk of the King's Works in Scotland and in 1730 Mason to the Board of Ordnance, a role that brought him the contract for Fort George (page 130).

His style included elements of Palladianism, fashionable in England at the time, but he was also influenced by continental Baroque and the work of Vanbrugh and Gibbs. Around a third of the 70 buildings that he designed remain, but perhaps his greatest legacy was the architectural dynasty he sired: his son Robert, in particular, came to be regarded as one of Britain's greatest architects.

Glamis Castle
Possibly dating from the 11th century, Glamis was added to in later centuries right up to the 19th; it took on its Baroque form in the 17th.

Glasgow: Holmwood House
Designed by Alexander 'Greek' Thomson and completed in 1858, this unique house blends elements from various sources, including Greek and Egyptian.

Glasgow: Pollok House
A classical Georgian house of the 1740s, similar to the style of William Adam but probably by Allan Dreghorn. Sympathetically refashioned in the Edwardian era.

Glasgow: The Tenement House
A first-floor flat in a tenement block, built in 1892 and virtually unchanged since. It was the home of Agnes Toward from 1911 to 1965.

Gosford House
Robert Adam's last house, begun in 1791. His domed pavilion wings were replaced in the 1890s with new wings by William Young.

Greywalls
Built in 1901 overlooking Muirfield golf course and designed by Edwin Lutyens. The house was added to in 1911 by Robert Lorimer, but Lutyens' curving façade remains unchanged.

Haddo House
A house designed by William Adam but built by John Baxter and finished in 1735. It was remodelled in the 19th century with interiors in the style of Robert Adam.

The Hill House
The classic Charles Rennie Mackintosh house, built in 1902 for the Glasgow publisher, Walter Blackie. Mackintosh's wife, Margaret Macdonald, collaborated on the interiors.

Hill of Tarvit
An Edwardian house by Robert Lorimer, designed in 1905 with a Queen-Anne revival exterior. Internally, each room has a distinctive style reflecting its use and content.

Hopetoun House
A palatial 18th-century house, begun by Sir William Bruce in the Baroque style, then continued by William Adam and completed by his sons, Robert and John.

The House of Dun
Designed by William Adam in the early 18th century, but altered in the 19th. Plasterwork in the saloon features Jacobite symbols.

House of the Binns
The home of a Royalist family, begun in 1612 and extended after the Restoration. Georgian reception rooms were added in the 1740s, with Baronial amendments in the 1820s.

Hugh Miller's Cottage
An 18th-century cottage and the birthplace of Hugh Miller, who achieved fame as a geologist in the 19th century. A Georgian villa, built by Miller's father, stands next door.

Inchcolm Abbey
Augustinian monastery, founded in the 12th century on an island in the Forth. The buildings that survive, many of them domestic ranges, are mainly 15th century.

Inveraray Castle
Designed by Robert Morris and supervised by William Adam, this unusual 18th-century castle is a fantasy fort that mixes Palladian, Baroque and Gothick styles.

Inveraray Jail
A Victorian courthouse and prison, designed by James Gillespie Graham and built in 1820 to replace an 18th-century prison by John Adam. Further cells were added in 1848.

Jarlshof
A site much settled through the ages. The earliest buildings are Neolithic, but there are also Bronze-age, Iron-age and Norse remains, as well as medieval and Jacobean houses.

Kelburn Castle
Possibly dating from the 12th century, the original keep of this castle was incorporated into a tower house in the 1580s. New wings were added in the 18th and 19th centuries.

Kellie Castle
A castle built round three towers, the oldest being 14th century and the youngest late-16th century. The building was carefully restored during the late 19th and early 20th centuries.

Kinloch Castle
A mansion on the island of Rum, built in 1897 in red sandstone. Fixtures from the early 20th century preserve an air of faded glamour.

Kisimul Castle
A castle claiming 12th-century origins, restored from ruin by the American clan chief beginning in the 1930s.

Leith Hall
A house built around a courtyard, with one range dating from 1649, two from the 1750s, and the final enclosing range from 1868.

QUEEN ANNE · EARLY GEORGIAN · MID-GEORGIAN · LATE GEORGIAN · REGENCY · EARLY VICTORIAN

ROCOCO

NEO-CLASSICAL
Robert Adam (1728-92)

William Burn (1789-1870)

PALLADIAN REVIVAL

David Bryce (1803-76)

William Adam (1689-1748)

BAROQUE

PICTURESQUE

James Smith (1646-1731)

William Playfair (1790-1857)

GOTHICK

Anne r.1702-14

George II r.1727-60

George IV r.1820-30

George I r.1714-27

George III r.1760-1820

(Prince Regent 1810-20)

1700

1800

Lennoxlove House
An L-shaped tower house built in the early 15th century, with the main range added in the 1620s. The house was restored by Robert Lorimer in 1912.

Linlithgow Palace
A royal palace begun in the early 15th century and added to by Scottish kings in subsequent centuries. Destroyed in a fire in the 1740s, it has remained a romantic ruin since.

Lochleven Castle
The remains of an early 14th-century castle on a small island in Loch Leven. Mary, Queen of Scots was imprisoned there in 1567.

Mount Stuart
A Victorian Gothic-style mansion, begun in the 1870s to a design by Robert Rowand Anderson and incorporating all the best modern conveniences of the day.

New Lanark
An early industrial centre, established in the 1780s. From 1800 it was transformed into a model working community by Robert Owen.

Newark Castle
A castle with gatehouse and tower built in the 1480s. In the late 16th century these early structures were transformed into the current tower house. Fine interiors survive.

Newhailes
A Palladian mansion designed and built by James Smith in the late 17th century; the wings were added in the 18th. Plasterwork by Thomas Clayton survives inside.

Orkney: Broch of Gurness
An Iron Age stone tower, once surrounded by several houses, with the whole settlement enclosed by a rampart.

Orkney: Corrigall Farm
A traditional farmhouse of two rooms – one used as living quarters, the other for sleeping. Suitably furnished, with box beds and a peat fire in the hearth.

Orkney: Earl's Palace
The palace of the Earl of Orkney in the islands' main town, Kirkwall, now in ruins. The Great Hall can still be seen, as can the Earl's own bedroom which forms a wing in itself.

Scots Baronial

Scots (or Scottish) Baronial style is a particular form of 19th-century Gothic-revival architecture. It was heavily influenced by the castles and other historic buildings of Scotland's Renaissance period, which dated from around the mid-15th to the early 17th century; typical architectural features of this era that were incorporated into Scots Baronial include towers, turrets, battlements and oriel windows. William Burn was one of the first major architects to start using such elements from traditional buildings in his designs, but it is his partner, David Bryce, who is credited with fully developing the style. Bryce's success lay in creating suitably castle-like homes for his clients without the inconveniences of living in the real thing: a castle designed by Bryce, such as Torosay (see page 154), was equipped and furnished for modern Victorian living.

The 19th century saw a growing interest in national identity in Scotland and a preoccupation with history and tradition. Scots Baronial became the style of choice for the country's newly rich entrepreneurs – when commissioning a grand new home to reflect their wealth, such men wanted a building that would establish their status as Scottish 'lairds'. When Victoria and Albert rebuilt Balmoral in Scots Baronial style, this further enhanced its popularity and henceforth its influence spread throughout the rest of Britain and even to the Empire.

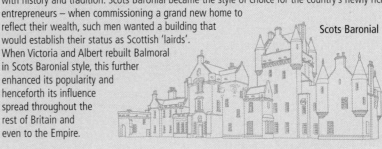

Scots Baronial

Orkney: Kirbuster Farm
Farmstead of the 'firehouse' type – a one-roomed dwelling with beds set in recesses in the walls and a hearth at the centre.

Orkney: Skaill House
House of the Laird of Skaill, built in the 1620s and added to later. Now maintained as a comfortable family house from the 1950s. The remains of Skara Brae are in its grounds.

Orkney: Skara Brae
A prehistoric village, the best preserved in western Europe and now a World Heritage Site. The village was covered by sand until revealed by a storm in the 19th century, with intact stone furniture

Scone Palace
Built on an ancient historic site, this romantic, 19th-century, Gothic-style mansion displays flamboyant interiors.

Stirling Castle
A Renaissance palace, inspired by European palaces and built on the site of one of Scotland's most important medieval fortresses.

Stirling: Argyll's Lodging
An impressive town house built close by the castle in the mid-16th century, then enlarged and improved over the centuries. It has been restored to its mid-17th-century appearance.

Stobhall
A house comprising several different buildings, added at intervals and grouped around a courtyard. The 14th-century hall, now a chapel, features an important 17th-century ceiling painting.

Torosay Castle
A Scots Baronial-style country house built in 1858 and designed by David Bryce. Restored to its Victorian splendour and preserved as a family home, Torosay is set in particularly fine Edwardian gardens.

Urquhart Castle
A ruined castle set on a promontory in Loch Ness. Probably the site of a Pictish fort, the castle remains date back to the 13th century. A 16th-century tower house can still be seen within.

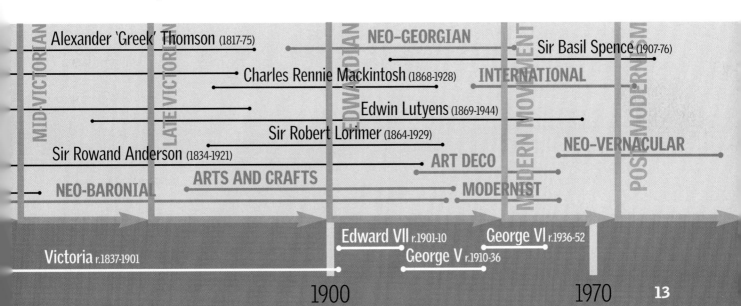

central

Blair Castle

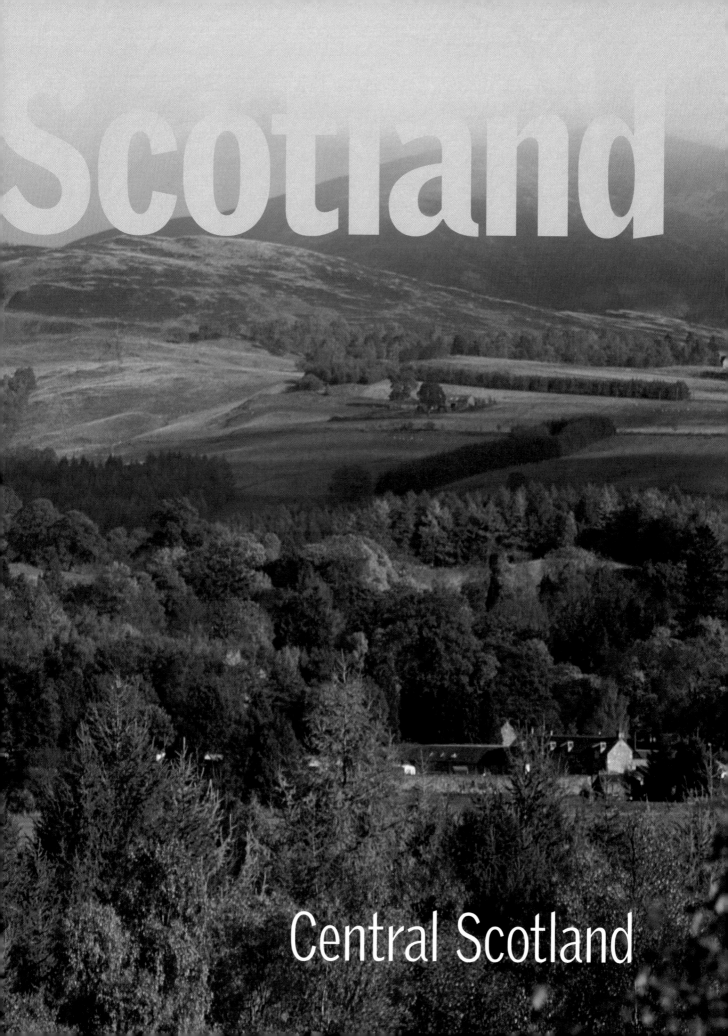

Scotland

Central Scotland

Alloa tower

☆ Remnant tower of a 15th-century castle

Near Alloa, 6 miles E of Stirling; National Trust for Scotland, open part year

A 15th-century tower is all that remains of the ancestral seat of the Earls of Mar. The castle underwent huge change at the instigation of John Erskine, the 6th Earl. Having helped to bring about the Union of Scotland with England in 1707, Erskine fell from grace for his part in the disastrous Jacobite uprising of 1715. Exiled as a traitor, he devoted his remaining years to architecture, designing flamboyant houses in defiance of the vogue for Palladian simplicity. During his exile, he reworked his own Alloa castle from afar. What survives is the only lasting legacy of his architectural career.

A model of the house as the 6th Earl envisaged it, with the tower embedded in a huge baroque palace, can be seen on the top floor today. There is genuine originality in the design, but he may at times have allowed his fancy to run too far – in the pond for fish, fowl and household water that he planned for the roof, for example. The Earl sent the plans to his son,

a man of more practical inclination who constructed a more modest version of the scheme. He tore down the stable wings and other old ranges, which the Earl described as 'fitt to be made a quarrie', sparing just the tower, 'venerable for its antiquity'. The interior was gutted to form a great domed stair, curving up to an open hall above. Most of what was built burnt down in 1800, leaving just the tower, which was then abandoned as a home.

By the time the tower was rescued in the 1990s it was virtually a ruin. The conservation work adds a new layer of interest; the medieval roof has been repaired with new wood and stainless-steel bolts. The furniture, silverware and paintings on display are on loan from the current Earl, who was the driving force behind the rescue. The prize exhibit is the cradle used by the infant James VI, who was cared for by the Countess of Mar during the exile of his mother, Mary, Queen of Scots.

Blair castle

★★★☆ Victorian ducal castle with earlier origins

At Blair Atholl, 8 miles N of Pitlochry; private house, open all year

Blair puts on an impressive show. With pristine white walls, it stands out against a backdrop of wooded hills, guarding routes into the Highlands through Glen Garry and Glen Tilt. A flag flutters from a battlemented tower. Visitors are greeted by a piper, or even, on occasion, by a parade of Atholl Highlanders, Britain's only private army.

The castle's history is swirling with romance. The oldest parts are said to date from 1269, when John Cumming of Badenoch took advantage of an Earl of Atholl's absence on crusade to build an illicit tower on the Earl's lands. In 1336 Edward III took brief possession while on a punitive raid into the north. A banqueting hall was added in the 16th century and Mary, Queen of Scots, was entertained there after a hunt that bagged 360 deer and five wolves. It was at Blair that the Marquis of Montrose raised the Royal standard at the outbreak of the Civil War. In 1652 the castle was seized by Cromwell's invading army and it continued to be garrisoned until the Restoration of Charles II.

In 1689 the body of Viscount Dundee was carried to the castle from the nearby battlefield of Killiecrankie, where Jacobite forces scored a victory over Royalist forces. Bonnie Prince Charlie was

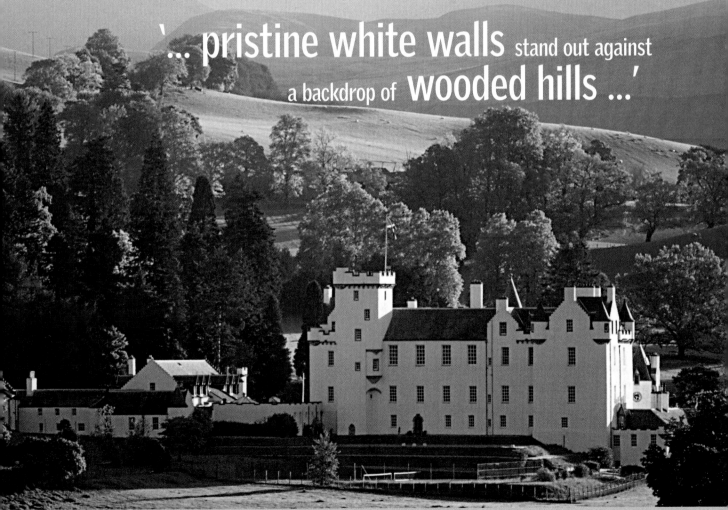

'... **pristine white walls** stand out against a backdrop of **wooded hills** ...'

Above Blair Castle boasts its own private army, the Atholl Highlanders. The regiment was raised by the 4th Duke in 1778. Right The Picture Staircase is decorated with plasterwork by Thomas Clayton. It was originally white and gold but was painted over during the 19th century.

there in 1745 and the following year, while held by government forces, Blair became the last British castle to be besieged. It was bombarded for a fortnight by the Highland army before they resumed their fateful march north to the final Jacobite defeat at the Battle of Culloden.

The castle is not quite the grand old fortress it appears. Some part of the medieval tower may remain and there are substantial 16th-century structures buried within the building. But Blair's baronial show is more an extravagant form of fancy dress. The 2nd Duke of Atholl, a Whig grandee, had no liking for ancient Scottish towers and after the embarrassments, both national and familial, of 1746 he decided the castle should be 'clipped.' Under the direction of James Winter, battlements gave way to a pitched, slated roof and sash windows were installed. Thomas Clayton, Scotland's finest plasterer, was brought in to create ornate ceilings and architectural details for new suites of grand apartments. The result was a ducal mansion, renamed Atholl House, that fitted the Palladian ideal of presenting to the world a façade of order and restraint, yet gorgeously extravagant within.

In time, such architecture lost its fashionable allure and in 1869 the 7th Duke brought in David Bryce to restore Blair's aura of romance. With a brand-new set of battlements and towers,

Above The Rococo drawing-room ceiling and cornice were created by Thomas Clayton, Scotland's foremost plaster of the mid 18th century, and are probably his most elaborate work in the castle. The marble chimneypiece is by Thomas Carter, who also crafted other fireplaces at Blair; a group portrait of the 3rd Duke and his family, painted by Johan Zoffany, is framed by the overmantel.

it became a castle for the modern age, complete with flushing lavatories and central heating.

Internally, the castle is a fascinating mix of periods and styles, with is layers of history reflected in the contents on display. The immensely tall, wood-panelled entrance hall is a baronial fantasy, with walls bedecked with weaponry and a stuffed stag lying glassy-eyed beside the fire. From here, an antler-lined corridor runs past vaulted chambers where centuries of history are on show, including an original copy of the National Covenant and the bullet-pierced breast-plate of 'Bonnie' Dundee.

The Picture Staircase is lined with family portraits. Of the 30 rooms on show, the finest are the first-floor dining room and the still more lavish drawing room, with a riot of plasterwork by Clayton. It is one of the first examples of a drawing room, rather than a dining room, being treated as the most important room in a house.

Elsewhere, the rambling mansion has a great deal more for the visitor to see: Mortlake tapestries that once belonged to Charles I; the 1st Duke's grotesquely flamboyant state bed; Jacobite mementoes; and furniture brought in for Queen Victoria when she and Prince Albert borrowed the castle in 1844. In the labyrinth of corridors and stairs, turret rooms and grand apartments, surprises are round every corner.

In 1936 Blair became one of the first private houses in Scotland to open regularly to the public. Now, with the 11th Duke living in South Africa, it is owned and managed by a trust with consummate professionalism. It may no longer be a lived-in ducal home, but it is a spectacular visitor experience.

Callendar house

⭐ A chateau-style mansion, now surrounded by a public park

At Falkirk, 12 miles SE of Stirling; museum, open all year

An ornate French-style chateau, Callendar House comes as a surprise. The approach leads through high-rise housing in the dreary suburbs of Falkirk. Then there is a glimpse of earthworks, the remains of the Antonine Wall, briefly the northernmost frontier of the Roman Empire. Finally one meets the house itself, with its mass of turrets, pinnacles and mansard roofs.

Callendar grew over many centuries, starting as the small medieval tower that still lies buried in its core. The owners, the Livingstons – later Earls of Callendar – added new wings as their finances allowed until, condemned as Jacobites in the 18th century, they lost their estates. Their home was eventually sold to a businessman, William Forbes, whose descendants continued to make changes, culminating in the French chateau in the 1860s. The low point for the house came in 1963, when, now owned by the local council, it was hemmed in by tower blocks, then abandoned as a worthless relic of a bygone age. By 1990 such attitudes had changed and an eight-year restoration began.

Most of the interior has been converted into offices and museum galleries, but two first-floor reception rooms have been restored. There is also a pretty, timber-vaulted library that houses the local history archive. But it is the basement kitchen that is the most impressive room on view. Dating from the 1820s, this huge, double-height space is equipped with original ranges, hobs and mechanical spits, all lovingly returned to full working order.

Castle Campbell

⭐ The ruined castle of a Highland chief in a glorious, spectacular setting

Near Dollar, 11 miles E of Stirling; Historic Scotland, open part year

Castle Campbell, originally known as Castle Gloom, stands guard above steep-sided gorges at the meeting of the Burn of Sorrow and the Burn of Care. The setting of the ruined stronghold is superb, poised against bare hills with a tumbling forest at its feet. The oldest part, a sturdy defensive tower, dates from the mid 15th century, shortly before the castle was acquired by Colin Campbell, the 1st Earl of Argyll. Campbell was a Highland chief whose main seat lay in the west at Inveraray (see page 133), but he was also a sophisticated courtier who required a lowland base closer to the palaces of the Stuart kings. By 1500 he had added a magnificent new range, including a great hall and private chambers, with windows overlooking terraced gardens to the south.

Further improvements followed around a century later, consisting of an eastern range above a pretty, twin-arched loggia. In 1654 the castle was attacked and badly damaged by Royalist insurgents who objected to its use as a Cromwellian garrison. It was left unrepaired, with later Earls preferring the convenience of Argyll's Lodging in Stirling (see page 41). The tower is the only part to have survived in some semblance of original condition. Roofed and partially restored, it contains a first-floor vaulted hall, with two floors of private chambers stacked in a second vault above. The upper room, originally the lord's ceremonial bedchamber, has an impressive ribbed ceiling decorated with a pair of grotesquely carved 'green man' bosses from which lanterns would once have hung.

Castle Menzies

✳ Historic clan seat, now restored

At Weem, 2 miles NW of Aberfeldy;
private house, open part year

Restored from dereliction by the Menzies Clan Society in the 1970s, Castle Menzies is a large, impressive tower house, part 16th century and part Baronial Revival. It was designed essentially as a domestic residence, with a few gun-loops and pistol holes as perfunctory defences, but still it was occupied by Cromwellians in 1646 and by Jacobites in 1715. In 1746 the Bonnie Prince himself was entertained, albeit reluctantly, by Sir Robert Menzies as the Prince's Highland army retreated to the north with the Duke of Cumberland in hot pursuit. The last Menzies in the direct line died in 1910 and the castle was subsequently sold, eventually falling into ruin.

The building is a good example of a Z-plan tower house, with a central block for the main apartments and subsidiary wings set diagonally at either end. An 1840s wing by William Burn is a respectful copy of this older architecture. In rooms that have been restored, the plasterwork and other decor is mainly 18th century. A death-mask of the Bonnie Prince is among objects on display in a collection of clan memorabilia. Considering that he ended his days as a sad old drunk in exile, he looks surprisingly handsome. There is also a massive broadsword that was supposedly used by an early Menzies chief at the Battle of Bannockburn.

With bright mustard-coloured walls and a red pantiled roof, Culross Palace forms an eye-catching centrepiece to one of Scotland's most picturesque villages. 'Palace' is misleading, since the Latin term *palatium* was used in late-medieval deeds for any mansion built around a courtyard. It is in fact a superbly well-preserved example of a wealthy merchant's home, dating from the early 1600s.

The builder was George Bruce, a minor laird with a precocious interest in industry and trade. Bruce began, as a young man in his twenties, by leasing mining rights and in 1588 he persuaded James VI to make Culross a royal burgh, allowing overseas trade. The coal from Bruce's mines was used in local salt-pans to evaporate sea-water; the salt was then exported to the Baltic, and timber was imported in exchange. Bruce grew richer by the year. In the 1620s one of his mines was a wonder of the age, extending for a mile beneath the Firth of Forth.

The house at Culross was built, added to and altered in tandem with the progress of its owner's career. The oldest part consisted of a kitchen and storerooms, with a hall and bedchamber above. Bruce's initials, GB, carved above a window with a date, 1597, mark the first addition, consisting of new wings to the north and south. Then, in 1611, a detached

Culross palace

At Culross, 7 miles W of Dunfermline; National Trust for Scotland, open part year

Above The withdrawing room was originally part of a larger room, known as the gallery, which was divided into two rooms in the 18th century; the wood panelling that lines the walls dates from this time.

three-storey lodging was built on the north side of the courtyard as accommodation for important guests. On this distinctly grander building the carved initials read SGB – the owner of the Palace was now Sir George Bruce and he wanted the world to know. James VI is said to have visited Culross during his visit to Scotland in 1617 and stayed as Bruce's guest. If true, this was a rare honour for a commoner without a castle, let alone a real palace, to his name.

After Bruce's death in 1625, Culross lost momentum as a town, failing to adapt to changing times. By the mid-19th century, the 'palace' had descended into an archaic slum: the census of 1851 recorded 16 families living in just one wing. The turning point came in 1932 when the newly formed National Trust for Scotland stepped into the picture, buying up and renovating buildings in the picturesque town. Bruce's house was comprehensively restored using documentary evidence, along with educated guesswork, and has been appropriately kitted out with furniture. A few rooms that

'... the barrel-vaulted Painted Chamber is a wonder ...'

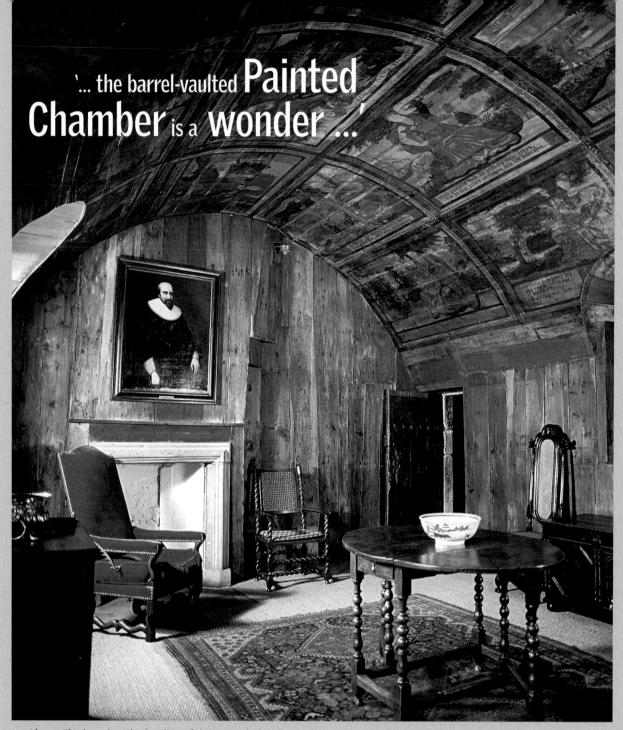

Above The barrel-vaulted ceiling of the Painted Chamber is decorated with allegorical paintings dating from the early 17th-century. Above the fireplace hangs a portrait of Sir George Bruce, the house's owner, attributed to George Jamesone.

were re-panelled in the 18th century are decorated in Georgian style, but most hark back to Bruce's day. Against all odds, much of the original painted decoration has survived from the early 1600s. Some was damaged by misguided conservation methods in the 1930s, but the barrel-vaulted Painted Chamber is a wonder to behold, with 16 naively painted panels depicting allegorical scenes with morally improving maxims underneath. The charter room, lying off Bruce's bedchamber, is more practical than beautiful and is evocative of Bruce himself. It has an inner porch of stone leading to an iron door and the room itself is fireproof, with a stone-vaulted ceiling and tiled floor. Yet it was clearly far more than a strong-room: the fireplace, window and ample space in which to work show it to be the inner sanctum of a 17th-century tycoon, the heart of his home and business empire.

Doune castle

★★ The fortress stronghold of a powerful medieval duke

At Doune, 6 miles NW of Stirling; Historic Scotland, open all year

The builder of Doune was Robert Stewart, the Duke of Albany, who was effectively the uncrowned king of Scotland from 1386 until his death, aged over 80, in 1420. Stewart was one of Robert II's 21 children and was appointed Governor of Scotland when his father became too infirm to rule. After his father's death he managed to hang on to power during the reign of his elder brother, the ineffectual Robert III, and continued unchallenged when the crown passed to his nephew, James I, who was held hostage in England for many years.

The fortress straddles a narrow promontory between the Ardoch Burn and the River Teith. It looks immensely strong within its curtain wall, and is entered through a gatehouse tower, but the large arched windows suggest that comfort was a consideration as well as defence. The castle consists of two large towers with an interlinking Great Hall. The gatehouse tower housed the apartments of the Duke and Duchess, each of whom had a spacious hall in which to hold court, along with small bedchambers and closets opening off a turnpike stair. The Duke's Hall was clumsily restored in 1883, but its twin-hearthed fireplace is still impressive. The Queen's Hall above is bare, vast and far more atmospheric. The Great Hall is equally bare and even more enormous. Beyond it lies the Kitchen Tower, with a massive hearth and ovens, and comfortable, well-warmed accommodation on the floors above. Behind the stern defences, the castle was designed for entertaining courtiers and visitors; in the Middle Ages, brute force and hospitality were both important keys to power.

After the Duke's death, his son and grandson were executed, the Scots redeemed their King's ransom and Doune reverted to the Crown. It became a royal hunting lodge and occasional prison, and in 1745 was seized in the name of Bonnie Prince Charlie. By 1800 it was ruined. The Earl of Murray's 1883 restoration may seem crude by modern conservation standards, but at least it preserved the building from collapse. Since 1970 Historic Scotland have been engaged in more sensitive repairs.

Edzell castle

★ A ruined mansion with an historically important garden

Near Edzell, 14 miles E of Forfar; Historic Scotland, open all year

Edzell Castle has one of the most intriguing rooms in Scotland, but rather than a roofed internal space it is a garden that lies open to the skies. As home to the glamorous, disaster-prone Lindsays, Edzell was built in stages through the 16th century. It started life as an L-shaped tower and ended as a large, well-appointed mansion, spread around a courtyard and flanked with a walled garden to the south. The buildings are now in ruins, for the Lindsays eventually went bankrupt – the last laird ended up an ostler in a coaching inn – and their creditors stripped their castle to bare stone. But the garden was merely damaged, not destroyed, and its elaborate structure survives as a unique and extraordinary work of the Scottish Renaissance.

The garden's creator was Sir David Lindsay who began to lay it out in 1604. Enclosed within high walls, his garden combined architecture, statuary and horticulture in an intellectual and sensory feast. Lindsay's original walls are still there, dividing the garden into compartments and portraying sculpted Humanist ideas: Planetary Deities preside over the east wall, Liberal Arts the south and Cardinal Virtues the west, all copied from contemporary engravings, perhaps with more enthusiasm than finesse. The plantings to be seen today date from the 1930s.

In the south-west corner once stood a bath-house, now sadly disappeared. In the south-east of the garden a small banqueting pavilion survives, with a circular stone dining table and spiral stair leading to a sleeping-room upstairs.

Left When the walls of Edzell's garden were built in the early 17th century, they incorporated a series of niches. It is believed they were intended as planting spaces, as shown here, and also as nesting spots for birds.

Falkland palace

★ ★ A medieval royal palace, restored in the 19th century

At Falkland, 4 miles N of Glenrothes; National Trust for Scotland, open part year

Its towers capped with conical roofs in the style of a medieval chateau, Falkland Palace looms improbably above the high street of the quaint little town that it spawned. The house was established as a royal hunting lodge by James II in the 15th century, one of some three dozen residences that the Stuart kings had at their disposal throughout their kingdom.

The buildings on view today, both ruined and intact, date mainly from the reign of James V. Between 1536 and 1541 he employed French masons to rebuild the palace in accordance with Renaissance ideas, perhaps to impress his French-born queen, Mary of Guise. Some none-too-subtle propaganda can be read in the design, with a fortified gatehouse symbolizing martial strength sitting beside a chapel that speaks of piety and peace. The most sophisticated decoration, with classical pilasters and delicately carved roundels, is around the inner courtyard. Given the early date, such classical finesse confirms James V's reputation as a king of poor judgment but impeccable taste.

In the 17th century the palace fell into decline and the east range was gutted by fire during its occupation by Cromwellian troops in 1654. The buildings continued to crumble until 1887 when John Crichton-Stuart, the 3rd Marquess of Bute, purchased the Falkland estate along with the hereditary position of keeper of the palace. Bute was immensely rich and a fanatical medievalist, already well-known for restoring ruined castles. He also built the extraordinary Mount Stuart on the Isle of Bute (see page 143) and Castell Coch, near Cardiff.

Bute's architect at Falkland was John Kinross, who saved and transformed the ancient structure. The Chapel Royal was respectfully restored and its original features preserved. But elsewhere, in the family's own accommodation, theatrical effect held sway, with ceiling paintings, tapestries and woodwork re-created with enthusiastic imagination. The bathroom even has a 'Jacobean' washstand. The library features elaborate *trompe l'œil* decor dating from the 1890s and is furnished with the clutter of later generations.

Glamis castle

★★★★ Historic castle and stately home

6 miles SW of Forfar; private house, open part year

Glamis Castle pulls out all the stops. Architecturally, it is a swaggering celebration of dynastic pride that grew from a medieval stronghold to become one of Scotland's most palatial stately homes. Socially, it is the built embodiment of Scottish aristocracy; indeed, it was the childhood home of Queen Elizabeth, the late Queen Mother. As a place of myth and legend there are sufficient tales of ghosts, monsters and walled-up chambers to bring a shiver to the stiffest spine. Combining all these factors, it is a premier tourist attraction, welcoming more than 100,000 visitors a year.

There were buildings on the site of Glamis from a very early period, serving as a royal hunting lodge. Malcolm II was, perhaps, assassinated there in 1018. Slightly later in the century, by Shakespeare's account, Macbeth was Thane of Glamis. More reliable history begins in 1372, when Sir John Lyon of Forteviot became thane through the patronage of Robert II. It was Lyon's son, also Sir John, who began the east wing of the present castle towards the end of the 14th century. By 1484 the Great Tower was complete, dominating what must have been a somewhat disconnected complex ranged around a walled courtyard.

A sense of order and architectural magnificence was established in the 17th century by three successive generations of the Lyon family, against a background of confusion and political turmoil. The building process was begun by the immensely rich and powerful 9th Lord Glamis, who was created Earl of Kinghorne in 1606. The project was

'... a swaggering celebration of dynastic pride ... the built embodiment of Scottish aristocracy ...'

Right The drawing room was once the Great Hall and retains a high, vaulted ceiling. Today, it is furnished with pieces from the family's collection of fine art.
Below right The ceiling of the Chapel is decorated with painted panels depicting scenes from the life of Christ. Portraits of the Twelve Apostles line the walls.

continued by his son, the 2nd Earl, who through his financing of the Covenanters managed to fall foul of both the Royalists and Cromwell. He died of plague in 1643, leaving his three-year old son burdened with enormous debts. Yet it was this 3rd Earl who eventually completed the rebuilding, while also salvaging the family estates. His diary, or *Book of Record*, is one of the earliest accounts of a renovation project undertaken by an amateur with big ideas and insufficient funds.

The Earl camped with his wife in the castle's only habitable rooms at the top of the Great Tower, and mused on the challenge of melding tradition with contemporary design. Against all odds he succeeded, after 18 years of effort. Despite considerable further works in the 18th and 19th centuries, it is still essentially the 3rd Earl's vision that we see today: a great Baroque chateau, topped with turrets, pinnacles and viewing platforms, fanning out from a central tower. From a distance, Glamis looks balanced and composed; close up, variety and restless energy prevail.

The drawing room was originally the hall of the medieval Great Tower. The most grandiose of the rooms on show, it has a ceiling of delicate refinement installed by the 2nd Earl and a huge fireplace of heraldic ostentation. Two paintings are of special interest. On the east wall hangs a portrait by Jacob de Witt of the 3rd Earl, dressed in 'Roman' costume and gesturing loftily towards his newly finished house, surrounded by his dogs and sons. Nearby, on an easel, stands a 1909 portrait of the 14th Earl and family, with their butler hovering behind. Among the children is the young Elizabeth Bowes Lyon, who would later marry the future George VI.

The Queen Mother remained devoted to her family home and retained an apartment there

'... romanticism triumphs over dull historical veracity ...'

Above Glamis Castle is home to many myths and legends. The Crypt is believed to have been the setting for a fabled game of cards, played between Earl Beardie and the Devil himself: the Earl lost the game and forfeited his soul. On a more prosaic note, during the 15th century the room was the sleeping quarters of the castle servants.

throughout her married life. Her rooms are now among the star attractions of the house, filled with photographs, nick-knacks and some rather splendid furniture, including the 3rd Earl's state bed.

The lower levels of the castle are the product of 19th-century medievalism. After dinner in the baronial dining room, guests might be taken through into the Crypt to shiver in the gloomy chill as they listened to tales of murders, ghosts and demons. Here romanticism triumphs over dull historical veracity, with suits of armour standing to attention against bare vaulted walls. The Chapel is more convincingly antique, with wall and ceiling paintings by de Witt that are superior to the artist's work at Holyrood Palace (see page 66). This is also where some visitors claim to have seen the Grey Lady, the ghost of a Lady Glamis burnt to death in 1537 on a trumped-up charge of witchcraft.

Hill of Tarvit

★ ★   An Edwardian country house of eclectic design

Near Cupar, 9 miles SW of St Andrews; National Trust for Scotland, open part year

The Hill of Tarvit was designed by Robert Lorimer in 1905 for the jute baron, Frederick Sharp. Unlike his near-contemporary, Charles Rennie Mackintosh, Lorimer was an architect who liked to please his clients. He was, in consequence, far more successful in his lifetime, but has received a lot less adulation since his death. The initial impression of the house is of a polite but rather dull Queen-Anne-revival villa, albeit on a splendid site. But impressions can be deceptive – this is an architectural chameleon.

An understated entrance on the side of the house allows all the main reception rooms to be ranged along the south front, opening onto the garden. Lorimer gave each room an individual style, reflecting the variety of his client's collection of antiques and works of art. The drawing room is French, even down to the carved moulding of its door, for the furniture is mostly Louis XVI. In the next room the same doorway is medieval linenfold in style, for it stands in a baronial Great Hall with early Flemish tapestries and 17th-century English chairs. The dining room is Palladian. The Library could belong to almost any comfortable Scottish mansion. Upstairs, the bedrooms open off a dramatic spinal corridor and there is a bathroom of Edwardian grandeur.

The panelling and plasterwork are superb throughout, for Lorimer had learnt the value of fine craftsmanship at his childhood home, Kellie Castle (see page 34). The paintings are mostly Dutch, and some are very fine. Tarvit is not a house to set the pulse racing, but that was not Lorimer's aim – he created a home to be lived in, not a masterpiece to be admired. He hated being asked about his 'vision'; it was enough, he said, to design houses 'in my sort of way so that they don't fall down'.

The House of Dun

✯ ✯ ✯ A William Adam house with famous plasterwork

3 miles W of Montrose; National Trust for Scotland, open part year

The House of Dun is a thoroughly seditious house – its entrance front alone breaks all the rules of Palladian design, rejecting English notions of good order. And this is just a foretaste of the decor to be found inside. The saloon, from floor to ceiling, is a call to arms, a stucco invitation to rebellion.

The house was built for David Erskine, a Lord of Session and the 13th laird of Dun. The first design was by Erskine's cousin, the 6th Earl of Mar, a former leader of the Jacobites who spent his time in exile producing wildly impractical architectural schemes (see Alloa Tower, page 16). William Adam was brought in to apply some common sense, mitigating the most costly elements of Mar's design. The house was completed in 1731, although the distinctive plasterwork dates from a decade later.

The entrance front owes much to Mar's vision. It is intended to be read as a triumphal arch, with a monumental porch rising right up to the level of the roof. There is a reference here to Scottish architectural history, for such arches can be seen at Craigston (see page 172), Fyvie (see page 181) and,

'... the porch puts on a **tremendous show** ...
a prelude to the **splendours** to be seen indoors.'

Right The saloon is decorated with plasterwork by Joseph Enzer. Above the fireplace on the east wall is a bas relief of Mars, god of war, surrounded by weaponry and symbols of Scotland. In the cove above is Minerva, goddess of wisdom, pointing to the Erskine arms in the cove above the entrance door. **Above** The head and claws of a lion can just be seen, peeping out beneath the overmantel on the east wall of the saloon.

although much earlier and cruder, at Hermitage Castle in the Borders. There is also Baroque French influence at work, anathema to English taste. Although entirely useless as a shelter from wind or rain, the porch does put on a tremendous show, acting as a prelude to the splendours to be seen indoors.

Joseph Enzer's plasterwork in the saloon is a *tour de force*. Both the high coved ceiling and the walls are a riot of symbolic emblems relating both to the family and to Britain under Stuart rule. The propagandist message can most easily be read above the fireplace at the eastern end. In deeply carved relief, Mars (the god of war and also a reference to Mar himself) stands guard over the regalia of Scotland, with an English lion squashed beneath a cushion at his feet. This wittily subversive fantasy was completed just two years before the brutal reality of the final failed Jacobite uprising, led by Bonnie Prince Charlie.

Aside from the saloon, few of the rooms at Dun remain faithful to Adam's design. The layout of the house was greatly altered in the early 19th century, when a succession of eccentric lady lairds held sway. It is their decor and possessions that are now displayed. The last Erskine laird was Millicent, who let out the house as a rather grand hotel. She left the whole estate to the National Trust for Scotland when she died in 1980. Following restoration of the house itself, the stables and courtyard buildings have now been brought back to life. Alongside re-creations of a gamekeeper's bothy and a gardener's potting shed, a weaver works at Britain's last surviving linen handloom.

Kellie castle

⭐ ⭐ ⭐   A medieval castle, carefully restored in the 19th and 20th centuries

3 miles NW of Pittenweem; National Trust for Scotland, open part year

Kellie Castle is a gloriously complicated building. It has three towers, all of different ages, with the oldest thought to be 14th century and built by a man called Siward, a descendant of the Anglo-Norse Earls of Northumbria. Some time later, with the castle owned by the Oliphants, a second self-contained tower was added, 50 feet to the east. Then, in the late 16th century, a third, southern tower appeared, along with an interlinking block containing a sequence of grand rooms. This was the work of the 5th Lord Oliphant, who as a result of the expense was forced to sell up in 1613. The buyer was Sir Thomas Erskine, later the Earl of Kellie, and the castle remained the family seat until the 7th Earl died in 1797. It was then abandoned, the last of its contents being auctioned off in 1829.

    The castle mouldered, its Great Hall serving as a barn, for almost 50 years until it caught the eye of James Lorimer, an elderly professor and a jurist of international renown, who had a young, highly gifted family. One of his six children, John Henry, was an artist. Another, Robert, became a leading Arts-and-Crafts architect (see page 31). From 1878 the family leased Kellie as their holiday home, living in conditions of decrepit splendour as they patched and painted the long-abandoned rooms, gently restoring the old castle with the help of a local architect, John Currie. The family stayed on after the professor's death in 1890, and in 1958 the freehold was acquired by Robert

Above left Towards the end of the 16th century, Kellie Castle was extended with a new range that linked its two earliest towers, providing a suite of grand rooms on several floors. Among these was the Great Hall, now known as the drawing room. **Above right** On the second floor, reached by a handsome turnpike staircase, is the Vine Room, named for the sinuous foliage of the plasterwork decoration.

Lorimer's son Hew, a sculptor. Hew carried out further restoration and in 1970 he passed Kellie into the care of the National Trust for Scotland, remaining as a tenant until his death in 1993.

The Lorimer influence is apparent from the start, with a Latin inscription over the front door that celebrates 'this dwelling snatched from rooks and owls.' An upstairs room commemorates the professor's considerable achievements and several rooms feature paintings by John Henry, for the most part skilful imitations of other artists' work. In the north tower, Hew converted what had been the medieval keep's diminutive hall into a private chapel. His studio in the stable block remains exactly as he left it, filled with unfinished works in his eye-catching 'back-to-gothic' style.

The house still feels like a much-loved home, its grandeur softened by the patina of age. The first-floor drawing room – originally the 17th-century Great Hall – has classical pilasters and a fine moulded ceiling, but the disregard for symmetry provides a curiously homely charm. In the dining room the panelling is painted with colourful vignettes of mountain landscapes and romantic ruins, thought to have been executed by itinerant Dutch craftsmen in the early 18th century. On the second floor the Vine Room features an ornate ceiling with a painted centrepiece by Jacob de Witt.

Lochleven castle

⭐ A romantic island castle once used as the prison of a queen

In Loch Leven, 9 miles W of Glenrothes; Historic Scotland, open part year

The setting of Lochleven matches the castle's romantic story. The sturdy little keep stands on a wooded island in Loch Leven, an eye-catching landmark that can only be reached by ferry from Kinross. Dating from the early 1300s, it is one of the oldest tower houses in Scotland. Its of a basic, square-cut form, with stairs and closets contained within the thickness of its walls.

The keep is now an empty shell and so, too, is the little tower in a corner of the courtyard where Mary, Queen of Scots was held prisoner in 1567. Her lodgings, though cramped, were far from grim, with a pair of chambers vertically arranged, the lowest featuring an oriel window that overlooked the loch. The island also proved far from secure – Mary escaped within a year.

In the 1680s the castle's historical associations and picturesque appeal attracted the attention of the architect Sir William Bruce. He aligned his own mansion in Kinross on the prospect of the distant ruin to create a thought-provoking vista spanning both space and time.

Scone palace

⭐⭐⭐⭐ A Gothic-style mansion on a site of ancient significance

At Old Scone, 2 miles N of Perth; private house, open part year

The foundations of Scone lie deep in history and in legend. During the Dark Ages, the site of the present house was, supposedly, a palace of Pictish kings and a centre of the early Celtic church. When Kenneth MacAlpin united Scots and Picts against the Vikings in the mid-9th century, he had the Scots' legendary enthronement stone, the Stone of Destiny, transported from Argyll to make Scone the heart of his new-formed kingdom. The stone was notoriously plundered by Edward I in 1296, but Scone retained its aura of significance and Scottish kings continued to be crowned here until 1488.

Following the Reformation, the old Augustinian abbey at Scone was rebuilt as a private house, yet still the sense of power lingered on. Charles II was brought there to be crowned in 1651, before marching to defeat in England. James Stuart, the Old Pretender, stayed there prior to his ignominious retreat in 1715. And in 1745 the Young Pretender paid a visit during the last Jacobite uprising. Today, Scone attracts a rather broader class of visitors with its mystical allure.

Given such a history, first impressions of the house are disappointing. Outwardly, there is no sign of the early mansion, let alone the abbey or prehistoric site. In their place stands a large, Gothic-style country house that would look equally at home on the banks of the River Thames, with arched windows, toy-fort towers and a castellated roof. And it is, indeed, a British house built by a British lord, the 3rd Earl of Mansfield, who was just 19 when he came into his title and estates in 1796. Although the scion of an old Scottish family that had owned Scone since the early 1600s, the Earl scarcely knew

'The interiors are **flamboyantly impressive.**'

Left The drawing room is home to many treasures brought back to Scone from France by the 2nd Earl, the British ambassador at the court of Louis XVI. The full-length portraits of George III and Queen Charlotte that flank the fireplace are by Allan Ramsay, a cousin by marriage of the 2nd Earl.

his ancestral land. His father had been ambassador to the pre-revolutionary French court, and the 1st Earl, though born at Scone, had specialized in English law to become one of the greatest jurists of the age. So when it came to modernizing the home of his ancestors, the young heir thought in English terms.

The architect was William Atkinson, who would later work on Abbotsford with Sir Walter Scott, and Scone is early proof of his Romantic sensibilities. In disguising and reorganizing the decrepit old mansion, he threw symmetry aside in favour of a Gothic dream that would become a prevailing theme of architecture through the 19th century. Far from being dull, Scone in its time was a house of startlingly original design.

The interiors are flamboyantly impressive. The Long Gallery – at 145 feet, said to be the longest room in Scotland – is based on the gallery of the medieval palace, which in turn must have been constructed from the abbey cloister. The fan-vaulted ceiling forms part of a decorative scheme that runs through the house, finding its finest expression in rooms such as the library, with its arched bookcases and carved oak doors, or more intimately in the Ante-Room with its stonework of

Above In 1842, the 4th Earl entertained Queen Victoria and Prince Albert at Scone. During their stay they enjoyed an indoor curling demonstration in the Long Gallery. Impressed by the display, Prince Albert agreed to take on the role of first president of the Royal Caledonian Curling Club.

intricate design. Many of the state rooms were refurbished, regardless of cost, in preparation for a visit by Queen Victoria in 1842. A whole wing was re-arranged for her convenience, since Her Majesty preferred to sleep on the ground floor.

There are magnificent collections of pictures, porcelain, ivories and furniture acquired through the 18th and 19th centuries by the immensely wealthy and well-travelled family, alongside less appealing trophies such as stuffed bears and elephant skulls. These sad, long-dead creatures share the Inner Hall with a stunning collection of Chinese and Italian Renaissance cabinets. The house itself can be viewed as something of a cabinet of curiosities, with strange and beautiful surprises to be found in every room. Among the paintings there is an intriguing Zoffany portrait of the 2nd Earl's daughter with her cousin, a pretty West Indian girl. On many levels, Scone upsets preconceived ideas about history, nationality and race.

Above The State drawing room has been re-created as it would have appeared in the 1680s. The original fireplace remains, with traces of the Earl of Stirling's arms still evident.

Argyll's lodging

⭐⭐ A Renaissance town house, heavily restored

Castle Wynd, Stirling; Historic Scotland, open all year

Argyll's Lodging is the grandest late-medieval town house to survive in Scotland. Constructed in the mid-16th century by a successful merchant named John Traill, it was later enlarged by Adam Erskine, a man who earned his fortune from the post-Reformation distribution of church lands. Further extensions in the 1630s were made by the Earl of Stirling, Secretary of State for Scotland under Charles I. The Earl died bankrupt following the collapse of his scheme to found a Scottish colony in Nova Scotia, and the house was acquired by the 9th Earl of Argyll, who enlarged it on an even grander scale. Argyll's career ended, like his father's, on the scaffold, but the house remained in the family's hands for a further hundred years. It later became a military hospital and when the army left in 1964 it endured the indignity of housing a youth hostel. Finally, it was restored by Historic Scotland and opened to the public in 1996. Externally it looks magnificent.

The restoration, based on contemporary inventories, shows the house as it was in the 1680s. Furniture, textiles and paintings have been reproduced, re-creating the state apartment of the Earl and Countess of Argyll. The result, although impressive, feels a touch too neat and new. The best bits are original survivals – fire-surrounds of weathered stone and faded painted decoration. The restoration has been undertaken with academic rigour, but caution has triumphed over flair.

STIRLING

Stirling castle

★★★★☆ Historic stronghold with a Renaissance palace

Castle Wynd, Stirling; Historic Scotland, open all year

'... a place **dear to Scotland's heart** ...'

STIRLING

Perched on a steep volcanic crag high above the flood-plain of the River Forth, Stirling Castle is both a stronghold and a landmark, the ideal combination for a seat of royal power. The site's early history is wrapped in legend; some have even claimed it as Arthur's Camelot. It was certainly a royal residence, comparable to Edinburgh, by the time that Alexander I endowed a chapel there in 1115.

Strategically, the fortress was of immense significance, guarding a vital river crossing between lowland Scotland and the north. Two great battles – Stirling Bridge in 1297 and Bannockburn in 1314 – were fought over its possession and within sight of its walls. In the 15th century, Stirling became the favourite base of early Stuart kings and in 1452 it was the setting of James II's notorious murder of the Earl of Douglas, whom the king invited to the castle for negotiations and then knifed to death. It is a place dear to Scotland's heart, redolent of history, national identity and gore.

No trace remains of the medieval fortress that once occupied the rock, for early buildings were demolished when the castle was rebuilt in the 16th century. The castle remained heavily fortified in an age of almost constant upheaval and war, but within its seemingly impregnable walls, the ancient stronghold was redeveloped as a masterpiece of Renaissance planning and design. James IV began the process in 1497, when he ordered the construction of a 'King's House' in the inner close. He built a new Great Hall, the largest and most magnificent in Scotland, and dignified the castle's main approach with an impressive multi-towered gatehouse.

A more ambitious project still was undertaken by James V, after he married Mary of Guise in 1538. His Master of Works, or architect, was Sir James Hamilton of Finnart, a nobleman who, unlike the King,

Mary of Guise
1515–1560

In 1537, Mary of Guise was an eligible marriage prospect for any European prince looking for a bride. The daughter of one French duke and recent widow of another, she was soon courted by both Henry VIII of England and James V of Scotland. She chose the latter and married James in 1538. Although she bore James two sons both died in infancy and it was their daughter, Mary, who inherited the Scottish throne on her father's death in 1542, when only six days old.

Mary of Guise continued to exert a powerful influence in Scotland and over her daughter. She also cemented the ties between Scotland and France, sending Mary to be educated at the French court. There, the young queen was married to the dauphin, the future Francis I.

Above The Great Hall has been recently restored. Its brightly limewashed façade has caused some controversy,, but it is generally accepted that that the hall appears much as it would have done when first built in 1503. **Right** The reconstruction of Stirling's oriel windows, overlooking the dais end of the Great Hall, was based on historical records.

had seen the Renaissance splendours of Europe for himself. Hamilton was also responsible for revamping the palaces at Falkland (see page 27) and Linlithgow (see page 82), but Stirling Castle was his masterpiece.

Departing from tradition, Hamilton laid out the royal lodgings on a single level, with apartments for the King and Queen arranged around a courtyard known as the Lion's Den. (There may have been an actual lion, but more probably, the fearsome king was himself the beast.) On the façades of the palace he set statues between every window, each in a monumental niche, with further figures on a parapet above. James V himself is there, as are Christian saints, pagan goddesses and classical heroes, along with a host of other men, animals and mythical beasts. Although the symbolism now appears obscure, its meaning would have been crystal clear to the King's sophisticated French bride and, equally, to educated visitors from England. It declared that Scotland, contrary to prejudice, was a land of wealth, culture and refinement. The spin did Hamilton little good. In 1540 he was arrested on a charge of treason and beheaded.

Within two years James too was dead, leaving the palace to be completed by his widow. Their daughter Mary, Queen of Scots, would hold lavish banquets there during her brief, ill-fated reign, as did her son, James VI, later in the century. But when James inherited the English throne and departed for the south, Stirling, like other Scottish palaces, fell into decline. During the Napoleonic Wars its

STIRLING

'It is **by far** the most
splendid hall in Scotland ...'

finest buildings were converted into barracks, their interiors ripped out or sub-divided. Even when the military finally departed, in 1964, the challenges of restoration appeared so overwhelming to conservators that the project remained on hold for more than 20 years.

Since then, the castle has been steadily transformed. In 1999 the Great Hall re-opened to a somewhat mixed response. The 'King's Gold' colour of the render is undoubtedly authentic, but looks rather startling on first sight. It is by far the most splendid hall in Scotland – the magnificent hammer-beam roof, as vast and complex as an upturned galleon, is a tribute to the skills of modern craftsmen. But sadly there is little historic atmosphere or sense of the past. The walls are covered with draperies, but no fires blaze in the five enormous grates. It has become a place for weddings and corporate events. Just across the way, the re-created kitchens are more entertaining, with sound effects, ghostly figures and tables laden with plaster fish and fowls.

The royal apartments are at present in the process of restoration. The plan is to re-create the Queen's apartment as it was when occupied by Mary of Guise, while the King's apartment will reflect the period of her grandson, James VI. It is a hugely ambitious project and great care is being taken with every detail, based on original inventories and contemporary designs.

The King's apartment should be particularly impressive, with replicas of the famous carved Stirling Heads reinstated on the ceiling of the Presence Chamber (since some of the originals are lost, a touch of artistic licence will have to be allowed). To one side of the King's Bedchamber lies a suite of tiny rooms that overlook the Lion's Den. It was here that the monarch slept, had his private study and entertained his inner circle of courtiers, mistresses and friends. Despite the grandeur of the state apartments, such intimate spaces lay at the heart of the Renaissance world. If their re-creation is convincing, they will bring one of the most ambiguous of kings back to vivid life.

Stobhall

⭐ A house of many parts, grouped around a courtyard

8 miles N of Perth; private house, open by arrangement

Until very recently, architects have played little part in the development of Stobhall. Rather than a house of coherent, planned design, it is a collection of assorted buildings that accumulated through the years, grouped in a pleasingly haphazard manner around a courtyard. The oldest of these structures, a chapel that may once have been a hall, is believed to date back to the 14th century when Sir John Drummond was granted the estate. A sturdy little tower, with lodgings on each floor, was added in 1578, most likely in replacement of some older range. Further buildings were constructed around a century later to provide more refined accommodation.

As Earls of Perth, the Drummonds used Stobhall only as a secondary house and were unconcerned as it sank into increasing disarray. By the 1960s, what remained of the house was threatening to slide into the gorge below. But then the 17th Earl stepped up as a saviour and renovated Stobhall as his home. Aside from patching up the existing buildings, he added a new range to house his library, architect-designed in a convincingly antiquated style. More recently, his grandson has completed a further programme of repairs.

The painted ceiling in the chapel is a most unusual variation on a common theme. Dating from the 1640s, it features Charles I alongside other kings of Christendom, including the fabled Prester John and, stranger still, the king of Mauretania riding an elephant. The ornate ceiling of the staircase in the Dower House is noteworthy as a piece of baroque splendour executed on a tiny scale. The drawing room, with 18th-century panelling and furniture, is intimate rather than imposing. At heart, Stobhall remains a home of unpretentious, occasionally eccentric, charm.

Below The chapel at Stobhall was converted into living quarters in the 1570s. In the 1640s the ceiling of what was then a parlour was decorated with paintings of real and imagined kings of Christendom.

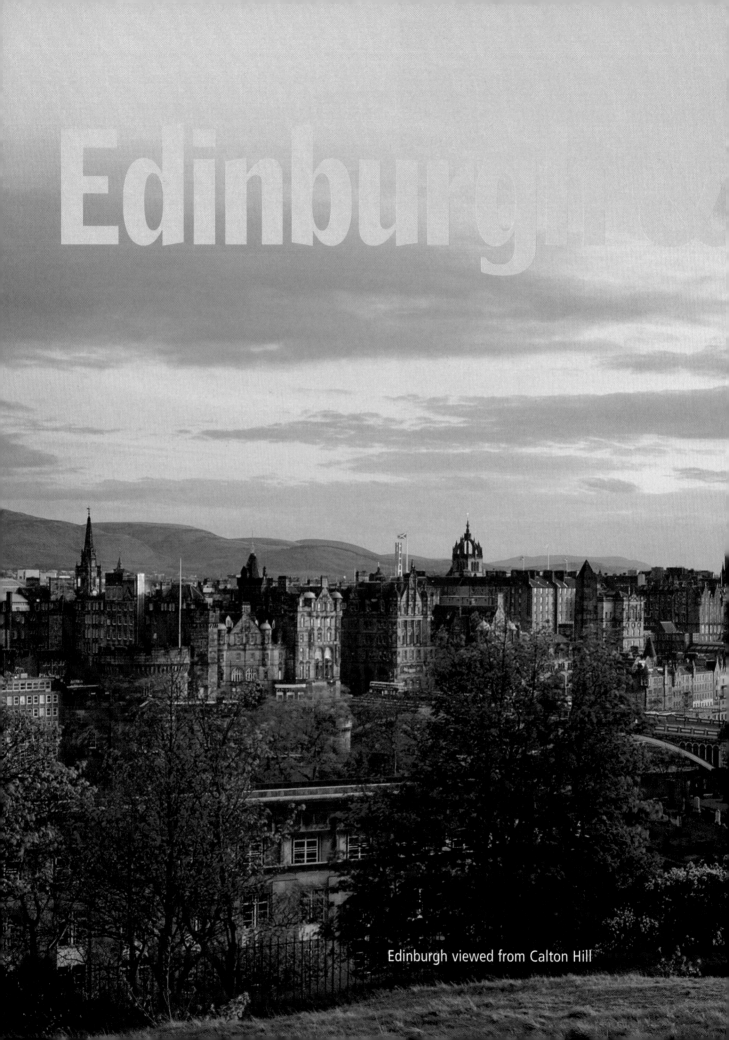

Edinburgh viewed from Calton Hill

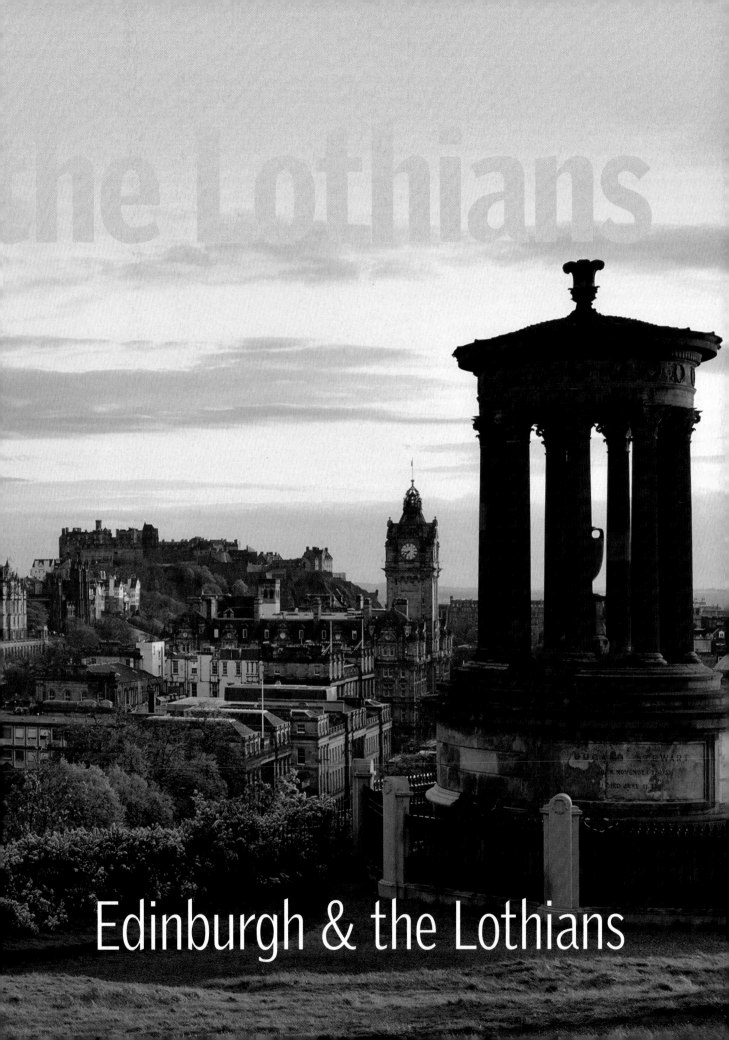

ne Lothians

Edinburgh & the Lothians

Arniston house

★★★ Eccentric splendour in an Adam mansion

Near Gorebridge, 4 miles SW of Edinburgh; private house, open by arrangement

Behind its simple, symmetrical façade, Arniston is a house of labyrinthine complexities. It was built – and is still owned – by the Dundases of Arniston, who were lawyers, so some might say unkindly that it is not surprising their home took years to finish, proved hugely costly and is difficult to read. The house is, above all, a much-loved and lived-in home, and over the years the Dundas family have fought a long and valiant battle against damp, woodworm and dry rot to preserve it. With rooms filled with books, portraits and mementoes, it is a place where architecture, history and personalities intertwine.

Arniton's story begins in the early 18th century with Robert Dundas, who, as Lord Advocate and later Lord President of the Court of Session, was part of Edinburgh's powerful legal aristocracy. In 1726 he commissioned William Adam to rebuild the family's old tower house. Adam produced a suitably magnificent design, but construction did not proceed entirely according to plan.

First, a pair of Palladian pavilions were built, with the usual linking colonnades. Then work

Below left Once the courtyard of the tower house, the main hall at Arniston was designed by William Adam in 1726 and adorned with magnificent plasterwork by Joseph Enzer. **Below** The drawing room was the creation of William's son, John, and Enzer's pupil, Philip Robertson. It was shut up in 1957 after the discovery of dry rot and not reopened until 1998. The original wallpaper did not survive the restoration, so the walls are now hung with a modern, chinoiserie-style paper.

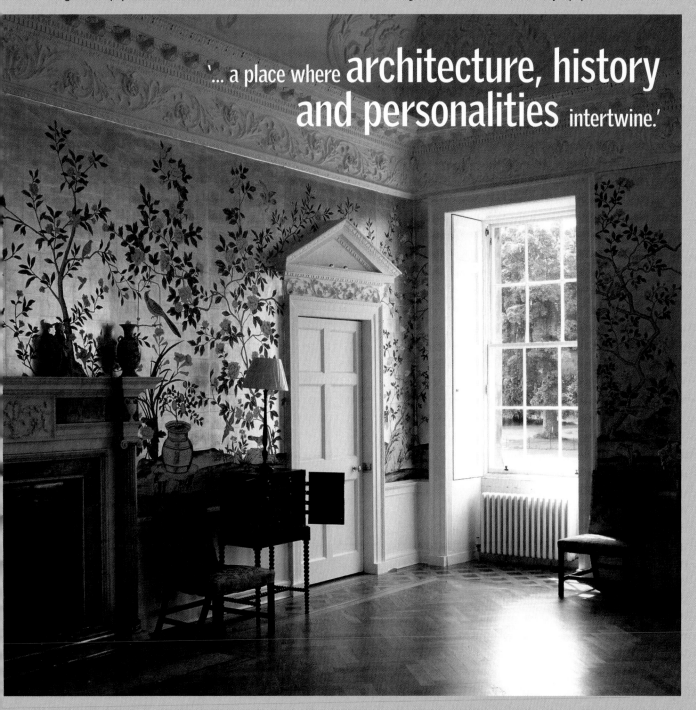

'... a place where **architecture, history and personalities** intertwine.'

started on the five eastern bays of the house. In 1732 the family moved in, no doubt looking forward to work progressing on the two remaining bays, which would provide ground floor bedrooms with a state apartment above. But then the money ran out. For more than 20 years the family lived with the inconvenience of 'a muckle great hole' dividing their house in two. It was not until 1753 that Robert Dundas's son – another Robert, who had the good fortune to marry a wealthy heiress – brought in John Adam to finish what the fathers of both architect and client had begun.

Above The upstairs library at Arniston is one of the William Adam rooms, completed in 1732. It was not unusual to find a library on an upper floor in an 18th-century Scottish house – such a position offered greater seclusion. The books were moved in 1868 when Sir Robert Dundas, the 1st Baronet, created a more convenient library on the ground floor. Today the display cases house the family's fine collection of porcelain.

The end result of this stop–start construction is a house that is undoubtedly beautiful, but has elements that confuse. The best feature is the main hall, the work of William Adam and his brilliant stuccoist, Joseph Enzer, always a formidable team. Rising through two storeys, with balconies sited above open arches on three sides, it is a room of spectacular extravagance that shows just where Robert Dundas's money was spent. Next door is the drawing room, designed by John Adam with plasterwork by Enzer's pupil, Philip Robertson. It is a fine room, but not altogether in keeping with the main hall, and its high, coved ceiling intrudes into the floor above, slicing window openings in two. Indeed, one part of the upper hall cannot be reached without a ladder. The state apartment was an out-of-date concept by the 1750s; it became instead a suite of modest bedrooms.

Blackness castle

⭐ An artillery fort and historic prison

At Blackness, 3 miles E of Bo'ness; Historic Scotland, open all year

Despite occupying a stunning location on the shore of the Firth of Forth, there is nothing pretty and picturesque about Blackness Castle. It is a fortress of brutally practical design. Constructed in the 15th century, it was a minor stronghold belonging to Sir George Crichton, Admiral of Scotland. Following the Crichtons fall from grace in 1453, the castle became the property of the Crown. A century later, its walls were reinforced and its southern tower raised in height to make it Scotland's strongest artillery fort.

From an early date in its history, Blackness served as a jail for political offenders. It held Covenanters in the 1680s and, later still, French prisoners of war. From the 1870s until the end of World War I, it was Scotland's main munitions depot. It was then restored as an ancient monument by the Ministry of Works.

Internally, the castle has been greatly altered, partly due to changes in use, but more radically by Cromwellian bombardment in 1650. The atmosphere of gloom is emphasized by heavy vaults and gun embrasures set in the massively thick walls. Prisoners in the central tower endured their loss of liberty in relative comfort, with suites that included closets and latrines. The smaller north tower, for those of lesser rank, offered no such amenities. At the lowest level is a 'pit', accessed only by an iron-grilled trapdoor and washed out twice daily by the freezing tide. The misery that its inmates must have suffered is beyond imagining.

'... a fortress of **brutally practical** design.'

Borthwick castle

★ ☆ An early tower house with a magnificent Great Hall

At Borthwick, 11 miles SE of Edinburgh, currently a hotel

With its massive keep standing guard above the meeting of two valleys, Borthwick Castle is a formidable presence in the landscape. At 110 feet from base to roof-top, it lays claim to be the tallest tower house in Scotland, and is certainly one of the best preserved.

A royal charter permitting its construction was granted in 1430 and the design is unusually elaborate for such an early date, with a pair of close-set wings projecting from the central block, divided by a narrow recess. The wings rise through eight floors and housed the kitchens and bed-chambers, while the hall and other important rooms are within the two high vaults of the main range. There are turnpike stairs, along with closets and privies, built into the walls. Aside from gun-loops in the courtyard wall, the battlements at roof level are the only defensive feature, but the castle's sturdiness

would deter most attackers. Borthwick was twice besieged – once by an angry mob when Mary, Queen of Scots stayed there in 1567 (she escaped disguised as a page-boy) and then by Cromwell in 1650. A deep scar high on the east façade is believed to be a legacy of his artillery.

For many years the tower was a ruin and avoided Georgian and Victorian 'improvements', until a sympathetic restoration was begun in the 1890s. Entrance is at first-floor level, past a guardroom and into the Great Hall. Faint lettering – 'Ye tempil of honour' – can just be deciphered high on the vaulted roof, and this truly is a cathedral of hospitality. An enormous stone-canopied fireplace dominates one end, flanked by tall, round-arched window recesses. In what would once have been the screens passage, a stone sink resembling an ecclesiastical piscina is graced with a delicate, fan-vaulted canopy. Guests might have washed their hands here as they entered. Cooking still takes place in the medieval kitchen, albeit on up-to-date equipment, and a former prison in the basement serves as the hotel's wine-cellar.

Crichton castle

★ The ruins of a medieval castle, with a unique Renaissance range

Near Crichton, 11 miles SE of Edinburgh; Historic Scotland, open part year

Francis Stewart, 5th Earl of Bothwell and the man who remodelled Crichton Castle, was a cousin of James VI and the nephew of the last, disastrous husband of Mary Queen of Scots. Highlights of Francis's picaresque career include imprisonment for witchcraft, attacking Holyrood Palace with hired thugs and an attempt to kidnap the king. It seems he was mad, bad and dangerous to know. But he was also highly educated and cultured, and the daring and flamboyance of his personality can be seen in what he created at Crichton. The outer walls bristle with turrets, gun-loops and other ferocious features, but the courtyard contained within displays an architectural sophistication that was far in advance of anything to be seen in Scotland at the time.

The castle dates back to the 14th century and the ruins grouped around its courtyard are the result of three phases of development. First there is the tower house, built by John de Crichton in the 1390s. His son, William, added three substantial ranges before his death in 1454. The remains of his Great Hall survive and it was clearly once a most impressive chamber,

with a massive, elaborately moulded fireplace. In Scotland's architectural heritage, however, such halls are almost commonplace, and that could not be said of the extravaganza installed more than a century later by the wicked 5th Earl.

Bothwell acquired the castle in 1581 and by 1586, when he entertained the King at Crichton, he had wrought a transformation that continues to amaze. Instead of the usual narrow, twisting turnpike stair, there is a broad scale-and-platt staircase, the first ever built in Scotland. Even more remarkable is the seven-arched arcade that turns the courtyard into a piazza. The most striking feature is the stone-work, cut in a pattern of enormous geometric facets. It is eye-catching and startlingly unique.

Right The faceted stonework of the north range is carved with such regularity as to appear cast from concrete; it dates from the 1580s.

Dalmeny house

★★★ A Regency-style Gothic mansion containing Rothschild treasures

Near Dalmeny, 6 miles W of Edinburgh; private house, open part year

The 5th Earl of Rosebery's marriage to Hannah Rothschild was the social sensation of 1878. He was a young Scottish nobleman, noted for his wit and taste. She was the only child of the recently deceased Baron Mayer de Rothschild and probably the richest spinster in the world. Wedding guests included Benjamin Disraeli (who was then Prime Minister) and the Prince of Wales. The union cemented the fortunes of the Rosebery family. It also explains why Dalmeny House, which became the couple's home, now contains one of the most fabulous collections of furniture, porcelain and tapestries to be seen in Scotland.

The exterior of the house is striking, if a touch bizarre. It was completed for the 4th Earl in 1817 by the architect William Wilkins, as a replacement for Barnbougle Castle, the family's decrepit old tower-house a few hundred yards away down on the shore. The style is English Tudor, a version of neo-Gothic that never looks quite at home north of the Tweed. All the battlements, chimneys and other such embellishments were prefabricated in London, using Coade stone, an early form of artificial stone. Elaborately fanciful, they give the house a fine chivalric air.

Inside, the staircase hall is also fanciful, with a great sweep of stairs beneath a hammer-beam roof that is actually plaster painted to resemble timber. Reception rooms are accessed off a rather pretty fan-vaulted corridor with 15th-century Flemish stained glass in the windows. But even when first built the house was described as convenient and comfortable, rather than stately. The glory of Dalmeny lies in the contents rather than its architecture.

In 1977, the 7th Earl decided to sell Mentmore, the vast Rothschild palace in the Chilterns that his grandmother had brought into the family a hundred years before. The sale of contents lasted for ten days and realized the then record-breaking sum of £6.3 million. But the best pieces were all kept back and taken north to Dalmeny, where they joined an already impressive collection in the house.

The drawing room is filled, museum-style, with 18th-century French furniture of superb quality. One of the finest pieces is a gigantic desk made for Jacques Necker, Louis XVI's Minister of Finance. From a century earlier there is an exquisite Savonnerie 'throne rug' bearing the monograms of the 'Sun King', Louis XIV, and his queen, Maria Theresa. On it stands a little table, with hidden compartments accessed by clever mechanical devices, that belonged to the King's mistress, Madame de Pompadour. Beauvais tapestries, designed by Francois Boucher, hang on the walls. The effect of such extravagance and craftsmanship is overwhelming. A portrait of Robespierre overlooks the scene with a disapproving glare. One can see why the age of ormolu ended with the guillotine.

The Mentmore treasures rather overshadow the many other fine things to be seen. A pair of delightful Goya tapestries, showing children at play, hang on the stairs. The Napoleon Room contains a collection of Napoleonic memorabilia acquired by the 5th Earl. The Earl himself pursued a political career and briefly, rather half-heartedly, succeeded Gladstone as Prime Minister before retiring to enjoy his race-horses and books. Such interests are also evident in the 6th Earl's private sitting room, which has a wonderfully leathery, 1930s gentlemen's club feel.

Below The drawing room is a treasure trove of 18th-century French decorative art. On the walls are Beauvais tapestries of Chinese-inspired scenes, designed by Rococo artist Francois Boucher. Ranged around the room are pieces made by some of the greatest cabinet-makers in France, including Jean-Francois Oeben, Jean-Henri Riesener and David Roentgen.

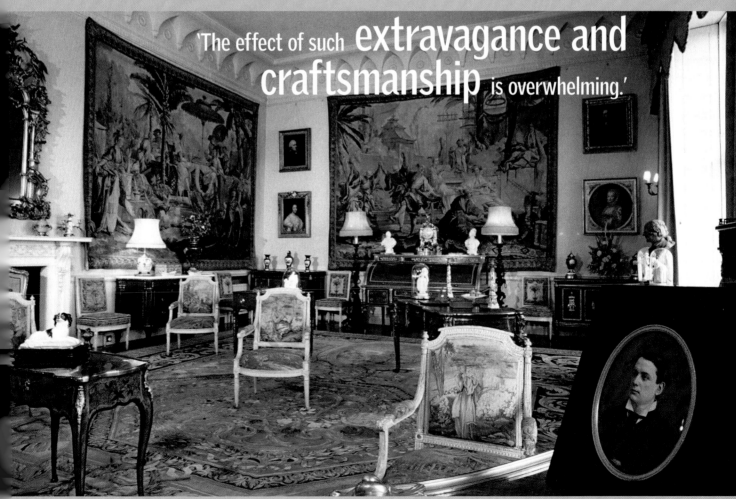

'The effect of such **extravagance and craftsmanship** is overwhelming.'

Dirleton castle

☆ ☆ The remains of an early castle and medieval house

At Dirleton, 2 miles W of North Berwick; Historic Scotland, open all year

Visitors to Dirleton get three castles for the price of one. Now conjoined within a single, sprawling ruin, each is a fine example of its type and an illustration of how domestic life in great households changed in the course of 300 years.

The original castle was built by John de Vaux in the mid-13th century. In the fashion of the time it was a 'castle of enclosure', with a sturdy curtain wall bedecked with towers protecting halls and other buildings within its courtyard. Stretches of the wall and a cluster of drum towers survive, as does the lord's hall within the largest tower, a strange, seven-sided chamber rising to a pointed vault, with stone benches in the window alcoves and a corbelled fireplace.

The castle was badly damaged during the Wars of Independence, when it changed hands repeatedly until Robert Bruce finally slighted its defences. Later in the 14th century it passed by marriage to the influential Halyburtons who, in the course of a century and a half, gradually rebuilt the ruins into a palatial home. The heavily defended gatehouse dates from early in this period. The vaults along the courtyard's eastern side are all that remain of a later,

massively impressive range. On the first floor the Great Hall has sadly all but disappeared, leaving little but a richly carved stone buffet to suggest its magnificence. The next-door kitchen, with twin fires and a towering vaulted roof, suggests the heroic scale of Halyburton feasts. In a still later tower, that lay beyond the high end of the hall, the family's private quarters were stacked above a chapel and a prison, with a squalid 'pit' below.

The last phase of construction came in the 16th century, when Dirleton was one of several properties belonging to the Ruthvens, later Earls of Gowrie. They built a fairly modest house into the medieval fabric of Dirleton, with large windows overlooking gardens to the west.

The castle was destroyed in 1650, when the Cromwellian General Monk evicted a party of Royalist irregulars who were using the old fortress as a base. In the 19th century the ruin formed the romantic centrepiece of gardens belonging to the nearby mansion of Archerfield. Gently besieged by flower-beds and topiary, the battered old relic of medieval wars is now a beauty-spot beside a peaceful village green.

Craigmillar castle

✩✩ An impressively fortified medieval castle

Craigmillar Castle Road, Edinburgh; Historic Scotland, open all year

EDINBURGH

Although uninhabited for centuries, Craigmillar is one of Scotland's best-preserved medieval castles. From a distance, its most striking feature is the sturdy curtain wall through which visitors must pass to reach the inner core. Dating from the 15th century, it has corner towers with gun-loops, a crenellated parapet and superb machicolations.

Beyond the round-arched gateway lies a pretty little courtyard shaded by an ancient yew. Ruined wings extend to either side and there were clearly further buildings against the curtain wall itself. Scorch marks on the masonry remain from an attack by the Earl of Hertford's army in 1544. Ahead stands the massive tower house that forms the castle's heart. Although its date is contentious, it is known to be older than the curtain wall and was probably constructed a generation or two after the Preston family were granted the Craigmillar barony in 1374.

In the 16th century, Sir Simon Preston was a loyal supporter of Mary Queen of Scots who stayed on more than one occasion as his guest. Following the Earl of Hertford's raid, he repaired and re-organized the castle, adding new accommodation in the wings. The west range as it stands today is later, dating from shortly after

1660 when Craigmillar was sold to Sir John Gilmour, a wealthy and influential judge. Sometime in the early 18th century the Gilmours moved to a new mansion on a less constricted site and Craigmillar was abandoned.

With so many phases of rebuilding, followed by years of neglect and the loss of timber floors, it is hard to tell how rooms were used. A 16th-century wheel stair links the east range with the older L-shaped tower, consisting of two double-height vaults with further chambers in the subsidiary wing. The hall, on the upper level, is a most imposing space, with a fine gothic fireplace gracing the high end. Further up the stairs, a chamber built snugly up against the chimney of a kitchen was presumably the laird's bedroom, but what would have been the purpose of the vast, dark and cheerless room above the hall itself remains something of a mystery.

The west wing built by the Gilmours, although in a ruinous state, suggests a totally different way of life. Well-lit rooms lead one into another, in contrast to the old tradition of stacking chambers vertically within a tower. Craigmillar, it seems, came close to surviving as a post-medieval home, but in the end it was strangled by its own defensive walls.

Edinburgh castle

★★★ Scotland's premier fortress, towering over the city

Castlehill, Edinburgh; Historic Scotland, open all year

The formidable heights of Castle Rock may or may not have been the site of an Iron-Age citadel, but there was certainly a royal fortress here by the reign of King Malcolm in the 11th century. Since then the castle has been battered, rebuilt and greatly altered, with buildings serving a variety of functions through the years. Of the buildings that have survived and are open to the public, in what is now Scotland's leading visitor attraction, the royal palace and the prisons are of the greatest interest.

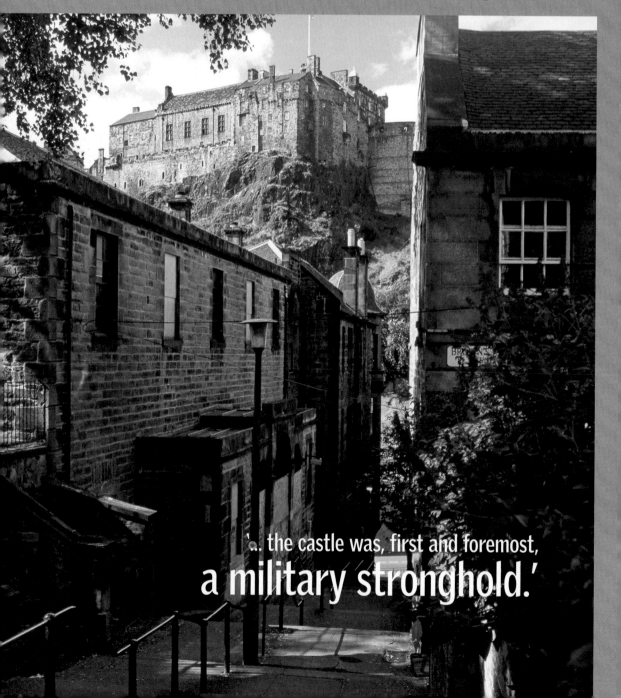

'.. the castle was, first and foremost, **a military stronghold.**'

The earliest recorded royal lodging in the castle was a massive tower house, known as David's Tower, built by David II in the mid-14th century. A Great Chamber was added in 1433, but by the reign of James IV this was deemed inadequate. In the 1490s the Great Chamber was rebuilt as a lodging fit for a Renaissance prince, and work then started on a Great Hall to form two sides of what is now Crown Square. To the east, the new apartments gazed over the city, no doubt a most impressive sight. In contrast, across the square they faced the workshops of the royal arsenal, for the castle was, first and foremost, a military stronghold. It was in this best-protected of royal residences, rather than at Holyrood Palace, that in 1566 Mary Queen of Scots gave birth to the future James VI. The birth-chamber was little more than a small closet, located off Queen Mary's bedroom, with a fireplace and window.

Much has changed in the castle since. David's Tower was destroyed during the 'Lang Siege' of 1571–3, when the royal lodgings were also badly damaged. In 1617, James VI paid a visit and the palace underwent major rebuilding. The King's birth-chamber was also redecorated; the royal coat of arms, featuring a cartouche of patriotic doggerel, was painted on one wall. After this time, the palace slipped into disuse, the last royal guest being Charles I in 1633. In the 1650s Cromwell converted the Great Hall into barracks, and the palace, too, was subsequently taken over by the military. In both cases, most of the original features were destroyed.

The Great Hall was the first to be restored, by Hippolyte Blanc in 1887–91. Although smaller than the hall at Stirling (see page 42), it is impressively baronial, but of interest largely on account of the weaponry displayed. The hammerbeam roof is the only original feature to survive (it was used as a guide to Stirling's restoration). The stone corbels on which the roof sits are intriguing, with delicately carved scrolls, winged heads and other curious designs. Dating from the early 1500s, they were probably the work of an Italian mason familiar with Renaissance forms.

Still within the royal palace, the Laigh Hall and its ante-chamber were restored in 1999, re-creating the 1617 decor. Aside from two late-medieval fireplaces, it is all the work of modern craftsmen, although closely based on examples found in other houses of the period. The bright

Above On 19 June, 1566, Mary Queen of Scots gave birth to her son, James, in this small cramped room off her bedchamber. Just over a year later, on 24 July 1567, she was forced to abdicate and her infant son became king.

Above Prisoners in the castle's vaults slept in crowded wooden beds. Hammocks hung from the frames above held any overflow.

colours and crisp finishes are disconcerting, but this is how the palace would have looked when newly decorated for the king.

Before work started on the palace and Great Hall in the late 15th century, massive vaults were constructed to create a level site. From an early date, part of this hidden labyrinth was used as a state prison to hold traitors, rebels, religious dissidents and other such offenders against the Crown. The vaults had two levels of accommodation: relatively spacious upper prisons, with fireplaces and windows, holding up to 40 inmates each, and a pair of dark, fetid 'pits', sunk into the bedrock, for offenders of the lowest rank. The first prisoners of war arrived in 1757, when the crew of a captured French privateer were landed at Leith in the early stages of the Seven Years' War. By 1763 further vaults had been converted to hold around 500 prisoners. Later in the century, large numbers of many different nationalities, were held during the American War of Independence, and there were at least 1000 inmates in the Napoleonic Wars. The prison then fell into disuse.

Two of the vaults have now been re-created as perfectly as film-sets. One replicates conditions during the Seven Years' War, the other is a 'rebels' vault' from the American War. Both are dark and claustrophobic, with thin shafts of sunlight glinting coldly off the cobbled floors. The conditions look grim to modern eyes, but were probably no worse than those on board a man-of-war. Another room houses a collection of artefacts made by one-time prisoners. These range from a fully-rigged model ship to exquisite caskets, carved from meat-bones in place of ivory, and, most cleverly, dies for forging one-pound notes.

EDINBURGH
The Georgian house

★★★ A Robert Adam town house in a sublime Georgian square

Charlotte Square, Edinburgh; National Trust for Scotland, open part year

Robert Adam designed Charlotte Square in 1791 as a grandiose culmination to Edinburgh's Georgian New Town. The same classical ideals would inform the city's planners for another 40 years, but the square's gorgeously decorated houses would never be surpassed. Bute House, the official residence of Scotland's First Minister, forms the centre-piece on the north side. The National Trust for Scotland acquired its neighbour, No 7, in 1966, a smaller and less extravagantly detailed house, suitable for a laird rather than a Lord. Its ground floor, first floor and basement have been restored to a close approximation of how they might have looked when newly built. The first owner of the property was John Lamont, a dignified but far from wealthy scion of a line of Highland clan chiefs, who paid £1,800 for his fashionable town house in 1794.

On the ground floor the dining room reflects the niceties of Georgian life. The cutlery is Sheffield Plate – the Lamonts, like most Highland lairds, would long have sold off any solid silver they may once have possessed. Each place setting has a single wine glass, together with a rinsing bowl for washing out the dregs between each course. The napkins have been folded in a manner established by research – no fancy fans, just simple squares. The sideboard holds a pewter chamber-pot for the gentlemen to use once the ladies had retired. The other ground-floor room, next to the dining room, is presented as a bedchamber. This was a traditional arrangement that remained quite common in the New Town's early years. Upstairs is the large, formal drawing room used for after-dinner entertainment, with a smaller and more intimate parlour next door.

Above The ground-floor bedchamber at No 7 Charlotte Square is furnished with a late 18th-century four-poster, complete with its original hangings; the bed came from Newliston, in West Lothian. **Below** The marble chimneypiece in the drawing room did not have to travel so far; it once stood in No 5 Charlotte Square.

In all the rooms, furniture and ornaments have been chosen to reflect the family's aspirations and their relatively modest means. The pictures, including Ramsays, Nasmyths and a Teniers, are perhaps too good. The Lamonts are more likely to have displayed kilted ancestors and prize-winning bulls.

The basement kitchen is equipped with an array of ranges, hobs, spits and ovens, together with the usual jelly-moulds and copper pans from the National Trust's seemingly inexhaustible supply. Visitors can also watch a video that dramatizes the Jane Austen-ish social life of the Lamonts in the New Town's Georgian world.

'... suitable for a laird rather than a lord.'

Gladstone's land

★★ An Old Town tenement with re-created rooms

Lawnmarket, Edinburgh; National Trust for Scotland, open part year

Few of the picturesquely gothic buildings in Edinburgh's Old Town are quite as old as they appear. Gladstone's Land is a genuine survival from the bustling, densely packed little city of markets, alleyways and tenements that formed Scotland's capital before the Union with England in 1707. Once marked down for demolition as a slum, it was acquired by the National Trust for Scotland in 1934 and has since been restored to something close to its original condition.

The street frontage, with a covered arcade and merchant's booth opening off the pavement, was added to an older building soon after Thomas Gledstane acquired the property in 1617. Town records indicate that each of the six storeys was occupied as an individual apartment, with the poshest tenants on the first floor, sandwiched between a cloth merchant and a minister. These are the rooms on view. The most spectacular is the Painted Chamber, with faded but still colourful designs on the ceiling beams and walls. The early 17th-century furniture is mostly Dutch, although the magnificent four-poster bed was made in Aberdeen. The re-created kitchen is convincing in its cosy squalor, with a clutter of obscure utensils and a 'close stool', or commode, beside the open grate. A further room, panelled in the 18th century, has been furnished in mid-Georgian style to reflect Edinburgh's so-called 'Golden Age', at the height of the Enlightenment and on the eve of the construction of the New Town.

Back on the ground floor, behind the merchant's booth, there is a re-creation of a 1950s 'back bar,' reflecting a time when part of Gladstone's Land was leased to the pub next door. Throughout the property, huge care has been taken with the decor, every colour being matched to ancient traces found beneath the later layers.

Left The Painted Chamber on the first floor at Gladstone's Land is reached by a turnpike stair at the rear of the house. The 17th-century painted decoration survives around the upper walls and on the ceiling beams.

Holyrood palace

★★★★☆ A medieval palace rebuilt for Charles II

Canongate, Edinburgh; museum, open all year

Scotland's last remaining royal palace stands close-by the ultra-modern Scottish Parliament, as though competing for the nation's soul. Both buildings send out a message to the world, but at least the language of the palace can be clearly understood. Combining Jacobean sophistication with a proud display of medieval roots, it proclaims the continuity of the Stuart royal house.

The palace grew out of an Augustinian abbey founded by David I in 1128 and rebuilt a century later on an impressive scale. Of these once-magnificent Gothic buildings, only the roofless nave of the abbey church remains. There were, almost certainly, royal lodgings from an early date and these were much extended by the palace-building Stuart kings, James IV and V. Just one of their structures has survived – a substantial tower built in 1528–32 to house a new set of royal apartments. During the 1560s this was a favourite residence of Mary Queen of Scots and, notoriously, the scene of the brutal murder of her secretary, David Rizzio.

The rest of the palace was converted into barracks under Cromwell's occupation and then suffered a major fire. It was rebuilt after the Restoration to designs by Sir William Bruce, Surveyor of Royal Works. The old tower was preserved in homage to the past, forming one wing of the new entrance front, with a matching copy added at the other end for the sake of symmetry. It is now hard for an observer to tell which tower is the original (it is the north-west tower, with gun-loops at ground level). Bruce's architecture is more dignified than thrilling, evincing a polite, classical restraint that looks a pallid copy of what was happening in England at the time. But there is much of interest to be seen inside.

'... a palace where **romance rules** over veracity.'

As things turned out, Charles II chose not to revisit Scotland, so he never saw the rebuilt palace, let alone used its opulent state apartments. These were decorated under the personal direction of his Secretary of State, the luxury-loving Duke of Lauderdale, a man with a passion for grand designs. After Lauderdale died in disgrace in 1682, the Duke of York (later James VII of Scotland and II of England) stayed at Holyrood in his role as vice-regal Royal Commissioner. A further spark of courtly glamour came in 1745, when Bonnie Prince Charlie briefly took up residence, throwing a famous ball before the Battle of Prestonpans. Over time, the rambling and increasingly ramshackle palace was colonized by members of the Scots nobility, who acquired chambers from Holyrood's hereditary

Left The bedchamber of Mary Queen of Scots lies at the heart of her private apartments; David Rizzio, the Queen's secretary, was murdered in the outer chamber in March 1566. **Above** The ceiling over the Great Stair was the work of the English stuccoists, John Houlbert and George Dunsterfield, done as part of the rebuilding begun in 1670. In the corners of the ceiling are angels bearing the Honours of Scotland: a crown, sceptre and sword.

Below The morning drawing room was originally Charles II's Privy Chamber; his cypher can be seen, borne by cherubs and eagles, in the plasterwork on the ceiling. In Queen Victoria's day the ceiling was coloured, painted to match the French tapestries on the walls. Today, the room is still used by the monarch for state occasions; the Queen receives important visiting dignitaries here.

keepers, the Dukes of Hamilton. For a number of such residents there was a particular appeal in the tradition that debtors were safe from pursuit within the ancient sanctuary of the abbey precincts. The last of these tenants were evicted, with some difficulty, by Queen Victoria, who made the palace a stopover *en route* to and from Balmoral. The present Royal Family remain frequent visitors, with the Queen hosting garden parties and receptions every summer.

This muddled history has not been kind to Bruce's plan, or to Lauderdale's decor. The original, Baroque progression of the King's Apartment was abandoned long ago; the sequence now starts with the Throne Room, where the thrones themselves look, rather disappointingly, as if they might have come from a pre-war department store. In most rooms, a leaden formality suggests that modern court events are seldom a lot of fun. But what remains of Lauderdale's scheme celebrates a very different monarchy in a very different age.

Of several ornate ceilings executed by the plasterer John Houlbert, the most spectacular is in the King's Bedchamber. The central panel, painted by Jacob de Witt, depicts the Apotheosis of Hercules (a flattering reference to Charles himself), with spaniels gazing on in admiration as the hero is elevated to the Gods. Working in a deliberately more 'primitive' style, de Witt was also responsible for the portraits of real and legendary Scottish kings that line the immensely long Great Gallery. These crudely propagandist images trace Charles II's dynastic claims back through 110 generations to a mythical King Fergus in 330BC (a more plausible Fergus was a king of the Dalriadic Scots in the 6th century, but even he was not responsible for engendering the Stuart line).

Public fascination with the palace has always been focused on the apartment of Mary Queen of Scots, preserved in the old tower. Even in the 19th century, the Duke of Hamilton's housekeeper was charging visitors 6d for a peek. The furnishings changed constantly as the Duke's discarded beds and chairs were moved around and strange relics were recovered from the attics. For many years, 'Rizzio's bloodstain' was a prime attraction, although the crimson paint has long since faded.

The last refurbishment was in 2006 and the rooms now look older than ever. Hand-crafted gothick-style vitrines are arranged as 'cabinets of curiosities', with copperplate labels describing their exotic contents: King Robert Bruce's skull is bronzed with age; the Darnley Jewel is a beautiful Renaissance pendant; and a suit of armour, according to its label, is 'traditionally Lord Darnley's (but not)'. There are tiny pistols belonging to the Young Pretender, the gilt place-setting of a later Stuart claimant to the throne and a Clouet portrait of Mary Queen of Scots. The connecting theme, though unstated, is the link between royalty, tragedy and glamour, presented with a hint of ironic humour. In the Queen's Bedchamber the ceiling paintings and decorative frieze are genuinely original, although the fact is scarcely worth a mention in a palace where romance rules over veracity.

John Knox house

★ A medieval town house with Jacobean decor

High Street, Edinburgh; museum, open all year

The picturesque old frontage of John Knox House epitomizes the appearance of medieval Edinburgh. The house survived Victorian slum-clearance schemes solely on account of its legendary association with the firebrand of the Reformation, but its antiquity alone now guarantees its preservation. The house is certainly immensely old. It survived the Earl of Hertford's sack of Edinburgh in 1544 and was rebuilt, with the frontage it still retains, in 1557. It was then the home of James Mossman, a prosperous goldsmith. If Knox ever did stay there it was during the last months of his life in 1572, when Mossman was awaiting execution for his support of Mary Queen of Scots and his house was under forfeit to the Town Council.

The Oak Room has 16th-century panelling and an extraordinary painted ceiling. Instead of the usual moralistic images and texts, it features a bacchanalian riot of star-signs, hawks and hounds, clowns, fruit and flowers, with a hermaphrodite devil as the centrepiece. Probably dating from around 1600, it was later concealed, remaining hidden until the 1980s. Time has faded the colours but a section has been reproduced as it originally appeared, offering a startling insight into Jacobean taste, gaudy and crude.

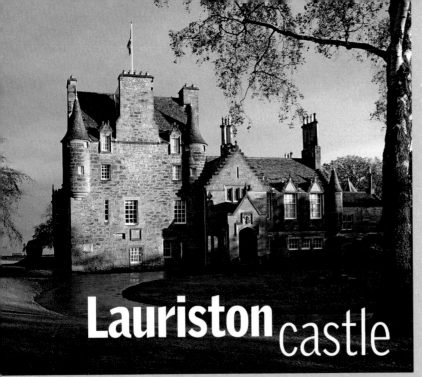

Lauriston castle

Cramond Road South, Edinburgh; museum, open all year

The main rooms at Lauriston have been preserved as they were in the early 1900s, when the house was the home of an Edinburgh businessman, William Reid, and his wife Margaret. It was Mrs Reid's intention, when she left the house in trust for the nation on her death in 1926, that it should be a monument to her late husband's taste as a collector. With the passage of time, the Edwardian telephones and bathroom fittings have become just as intriguing for modern visitors as any of the fine objects to be seen on display.

Part of the house is very old indeed, consisting of a tower built in 1593. This was modernized and extended in 1825 by William Burn for Thomas Allan, a banker, newspaper proprietor and friend of Sir Walter Scott. There is, perhaps, a hint of Abbotsford in the design. There were more additions in the 19th century and a major refurbishment when the Reids arrived. Mr Reid's acquisitive obsessions were diverse – mezzotint prints, Eastern rugs, Sheffield plate and tapestries known as 'Crossley Wool Mosaics' were hunted down through salerooms with predatory zeal and brought back, like trophies, to his home. In the time-warp atmosphere, it is almost as if ghosts are waiting for modern visitors to leave.

Above When William Reid bought Lauriston Castle in 1902 he set about refurnishing the rooms. The library houses part of his collection of books, prints and *objets d'art*. As proprietor of a leading Edinburgh firm of cabinet-makers, Reid was well placed to acquire several fine pieces of furniture.

EDIN

Mary King's close

BURGH

Warriston's Close, Edinburgh;
museum, open all year

For generations, tales about Mary King's Close formed part of Edinburgh's folklore. It was said that the street's inhabitants had been left to starve when infected with the plague and that their homes were then buried. There were stories of ghostly apparitions and unearthly sounds.

The truth is more prosaic, but nonetheless strange. When the City Chambers were constructed in the mid-18th century (originally as a merchants' exchange), a medieval warren of narrow, steeply sloping lanes was cleared. But the houses were not razed to the ground. Instead, their lower storeys were entombed within a vaulted platform that supported the huge new building above. As the City Chambers were extended, what remained of the closes further down the hill also disappeared, until there was nothing on the surface to be seen. Deep beneath the Council Chambers the cobbled alleys, house fronts, doorways and rooms still remained, abandoned.

Costumed guides, many of them 'resting' actors, now take visitors around this eerie lost domain, telling of the people – including Mary King herself – who once lived, worked and died in what are now the skeletal remains of homes. Aside from a few plague-ridden mannequins the presentation is low-key and there is not a huge amount to see. But the lack of restoration adds to the sense of history, which is almost tangible. And then there are the ghosts. One is a little girl and visitors leave cuddly toys in her room. In Mary King's Close, disbelief is best left upstairs in the modern world.

Gosford house

★ ★ ★ Robert Adam's flawed final masterpiece, overlooking the Forth, with a fine art collection

Near Longniddry, 14 miles E of Edinburgh; private house, open part year

Gosford is the flawed architectural masterpiece of Robert Adam's last years. Designed for the 7th Earl of Wemyss, it was an ambitious project intended to provide a suitable home for the Earl's art collection. Particular attention was paid to the windows, to get the light just right for pictures to be hung there. Adam died in 1792, a year after building began.

The first phase of construction was complete by 1800, but it did not stay that way for long. The 7th Earl never actually lived there, and his grandson, who succeeded him as 8th Earl in 1808, had Adam's domed pavilion wings torn down, leaving a shorn central block. The 9th Earl would have been happy to tear down the rest, but the house found a champion in his son, Francis Richard Charteris, who inherited his great-great-grandfather's love of art. He added substantially to the collection, particularly during his travels to Italy.

Francis became 10th Earl in 1883, and in the 1890s he commissioned the architect William Young to breathe new life into Gosford House. He rebuilt the wings and remodelled the entrance, creating the superb double staircase that sweeps up to a gallery with a balustrade of pink alabaster and elaborately carved Venetian arches. The drawing room here overlooks the marble hall, an immense and elegant space topped by an enormous central dome. It is rather like the palace of a Roman emperor, translated from the Adriatic to the Firth of Forth.

Until the Earl's death, in 1914, the house enjoyed a period as a family home, then after World War I it had a brief stint as a hotel. In 1940, while occupied by the army, fire struck the central block, damaging several rooms and the roof. The later discovery of dry rot meant removal of an even larger chunk of roof, leaving much of the house a ravaged shell. Bravely, in 1951, the 12th Earl took up permanent residence in the south wing and began the massive task of restoring Gosford.

The family rooms are now comfortable, and although a daunting amount remains to be done, the rooms in Adam's central block have been returned to usable condition. The roof was put back in 1987 and the cavernous galleries and halls are now plastered. In addition to the art collection, some pieces of furniture are outstanding, notably two 17th-century Dutch marquetry cabinets. There is also a sideboard the size of a cathedral altar, so monumentally absurd it takes the breath away. In practically all respects, Gosford goes in for extremes.

Right At the end of the 19th century, the architect William Young designed a new entrance hall for Gosford House. Venetian arches look down over the massive double staircase that leads up to the gallery.
Below The 10th Earl of Wemyss, Young's patron at Gosford, was a keen collector of fine art and the top-lit gallery became the perfect setting for works by artists such as Botticelli, Rubens, Murillo and Ruisdael.

Greywalls

⭐ An arts-and-crafts country house by Lutyens, enlarged by Lorimer

At Gullane, 20 miles E of Edinburgh; now a hotel

Edwin Lutyens was a very English architect. On a domestic level, often working in collaboration with the garden designer Gertrude Jekyll, he produced superbly crafted manor houses that answered an Edwardian dream of mellow stone and croquet lawns. Aside from the conversion of an old inn on the Firth of Clyde, Greywalls is the sole example of his work in Scotland.

The house was built in 1901 as the holiday home of Alfred Lyttleton, a politician and keen sportsman. It occupies a superb site on the edge of Muirfield golf course, with views across the Firth of Forth, and was designed for comfort rather than show. It was enlarged by Robert Lorimer in 1911 and then acquired in 1924 by Sir James Horlick, whose descendants have run it for the past 60 years as a country-house hotel.

Lutyens' curvaceous entrance front remains essentially unchanged – unassumingly simple, yet subtly detailed. Two of the original reception rooms display great originality and charm. The first is a gallery that forms the axis of the house from front to rear, with light streaming in from the garden terrace to one side. From here, a vista leads through arches to the library, a spacious yet cosy panelled room, unaltered since the 1920s, that is perfect for afternoons too wet for a round of golf. There are battered old who-dunnits on the shelves, a piano and a wind-up gramophone. Such details may be contrived for the amusement of guests, but they still help Greywalls be a delightfully convincing evocation of a pre-war country-house idyll.

Hopetoun house

★★★★☆ A magnificent 18th-century stately home

At South Queensferry, 12 miles W of Edinburgh; private house, open part year

Hopetoun is the grandest of Scotland's classical country houses. In terms of architecture, scale and setting, it ranks with Castle Howard or Kedleston, and like those English cousins, it was built as a statement of wealth, good taste and prestige. The story of Hopetoun's building is in many ways as fascinating as the house itself, involving extravagance, obsession and insecurity on an heroic scale. The project spanned more than 50 years, over the course of which the house was ambitiously extended and then, just a few years later, partially demolished and completely redesigned. All this was due to the perfectionism of Hopetoun's first owner, the immensely wealthy Charles Hope.

The Hopes had risen fast from relatively humble origins as Edinburgh merchants in the 16th century. By the 1650s, Sir James Hope was a Lord of Session, Master of the Scottish Mint and, through his heiress wife, the owner of lead-mines in Lanarkshire. His son, John Hope, married an aristocrat, Lady Margaret Hamilton, and purchased an estate at Abercorn where he planned to build a mansion. But in 1682, before the house was started, John was drowned in a shipwreck, leaving his one-year old son Charles as his heir. It was Charles's mother, Margaret, who first commissioned a design for Hopetoun House when her son reached 17, engaging the services of Sir William Bruce, Scotland's best-established and most gentlemanly architect of the day.

The first incarnation of Hopetoun was an unpretentious four-square house, with apartments ranged around a central octagonal great stair, which can still be seen at the heart of the house today. Before the building was finished Charles had come of age and married a daughter of the Earl of Anandale, which took him into the highest ranks of Scots nobility. In 1703 he was himself created

Below Hopetoun's Red Drawing Room is one of the state rooms created by William Adam. The original red damask, purchased in 1766, still covers the walls. Contemporary console tables made by James Cullen stand between the windows. Right The Yellow Drawing Room, like the Red, was decorated by William's son, John; it was originally a dining room. The plasterwork ceilings of both drawing rooms were the work of John Dawson, a stuccoist discovered by John Adam.

'It is certainly a
stupendous piece of work.'

Earl of Hopetoun. The home that his mother had considered suitable was clearly quite inadequate for a nobleman of such celebrity, so Hopetoun House was radically extended, again with Bruce as architect. It was illustrated in *Vitruvius Britannicus* in 1715 – a Baroque palace with unusual convex colonnades linked to pavilion wings on either side. John Macky described it in his *Journey through Scotland*, published in 1723, as 'much the finest seat in Britain'. But still the Earl was not satisfied. His problem may have been the roof; it was hipped and visible, unlike most country seats that featured in *Vitruvius Britannicus*, which had seemingly flat roofs concealed behind balustrades. Worse still, none apart from Hopetoun had convex colonnades.

In 1721 the Earl had turned to William Adam, then a rapidly rising architectural star. Adam was to work on Hopetoun for more than a quarter of a century. He designed a new entrance front, extending Bruce's house with long, linear apartments to each side. Adam was still in charge of the project when he died in 1748, leaving his sons, John and Robert, to complete the main façade and fit out the rooms. By then Charles Hope too was dead and it was his son, the 2nd Earl, who in late middle age had the pleasure of seeing the scaffolding removed and the plasterers and painters finally finish and move out.

The end result is certainly a stupendous piece of work. The 17-bay frontage, with giant Corinthian pilasters, is an uncompromising statement of grandeur that rises up from the landscape to greet its visitors. The colonnades that frame this monumental view, reformed by Adam into concave curves, lead to pavilions that are each the size of a substantial house. The northern pavilion was devoted to Hope's stables, said to be the finest in the land, while its

'... Bruce's **octagonal staircase hall** is the **most attractive** room in the house.'

Above In 1984, the cupola over the stairs at Hopetoun was found to contain 18th-century murals, which had been painted over at the turn of the 20th century to conceal rainwater damage. The paintings represent the rise of the Hopes to the aristocracy. Angels bear aloft their coat of arms, and an earl's coronet, supported by cherubs, is set above the family motto: '*At spes non fructa*' – 'But hope is not broken'.

southern partner was intended as a library and laboratory, as befitted a nobleman of the Enlightenment. This was all the work of Adam and his sons. Bruce's mansion can still be seen from the rear, where his central block of seven bays remains virtually unchanged.

Behind its unified façade Hopetoun is really two great houses melded into one, offering a sometimes startling contrast in styles. Leading off the entrance hall, the enfilade of state rooms is by William Adam with decor by his sons, They are, as one would expect, superbly grand, with the Red Drawing Room featuring a particularly sumptuous ceiling. In contrast, the wood-panelled rooms in Bruce's block belong to an earlier, less pretentious world. Bruce's octagonal staircase hall is the most attractive room in the house. It has exquisite carvings by Alexander Eizat, who had worked with Bruce at Holyrood, and a painted cupola that represents the apotheosis of the Hope family into aristocracy and heaven. The murals up the stairs themselves are modern, painted by William McLaren in 1967; although initially surprising, they fit in rather well.

Throughout the house there are paintings of the highest quality, many of them portraits of the family. In the dining room, the 1st Earl is shown studying a plan of the house, with its half-built façade behind, suggesting his influence over the design. In the Red Drawing Room there is a pretty Canaletto of the Doge's Palace, and in pride of place above the fire, a sternly frowning doge representing the ideal of a mercantile aristocracy.

House of the Binns

★ ★ A Restoration house with Georgian interiors

Near Linlithgow, 15 miles W of Edinburgh; National Trust for Scotland, open part year

Cantankerous, quixotic and unflinching in their principles, the Dalyells have always fought their enemies with gusto, from Cromwell in the 1640s to Margaret Thatcher in the 1980s. The House of the Binns has been their home for the past 400 years and the building's history has mirrored their tumultuous lives.

The house was begun sometime after 1612 by Thomas Dalyell, a wealthy merchant and adviser to James VI. His son, General Sir Tam Dalyell, achieved almost legendary stature on the Royalist side during the Civil War and in the religious conflicts that came after. He escaped into exile and the service of the Russian tsar, but returned on Charles II's Restoration in 1660. Denounced by his enemies as a 'Muscovite Devil' whose home would surely be blown down, his response was to add the west wing, declaring: 'I will build me a turret at every corner to pin down my walls.'

The house survived, and in the 1740s new reception rooms were built out over the courtyard by Sir Robert Dalyell, the 4th Baronet.

Finally, in the 1820s, the whole place was given a Baronial make-over, with battlements tacked on to every wall possible.

Inside, the house remains very much a lived-in home. There is no single, overriding 'style'. Instead, decor has been altered by degrees and furniture has simply accumulated through the years. The shade of old Sir Tam is conjured up at every turn with portraits, personal possessions and mementoes. In the dining room are his bible, dirk and comb (he refused to trim his hair or beard until the Restoration). His riding boots can also be seen – according to his enemies, they could bring cold water to a boil.

Equally in evidence are the photographs, political cartoons and personal possessions of the current occupant, the retired Labour MP, Tam Dalyell. His mother, Eleanor Dalyell, gave the house to the National Trust for Scotland in 1944, with the proviso that the family be permitted to remain. She also retained a claim to any treasure found buried in the grounds. The Binns is a house of legends, secrets and tall tales.

Inchcolm abbey

★ An isolated island monastery, with well-preserved domestic buildings

In the Firth of Forth, 8 miles NW of Edinburgh; Historic Scotland, open part year

A sense of mystery clings like sea-mist to the lonely island abbey of Inchcolm. Like Iona in the west, it may once have been a centre for St Columba's missionaries. It was certainly considered hallowed ground by the 11th century, when Danish warriors were buried there. In 1123, Alexander I and a shipload of companions were stranded on the island by a storm and shared the provisions of its resident hermit. This act of generosity subsequently led to the royal foundation of an Augustinian monastery in the reign of David I. The old hermit's cell can still be seen – a small, cave-like chamber that appears to have been heavily restored in a late-medieval conservation project.

The rest of the abbey buildings are mostly 15th century, dating from a major reconstruction after damage caused by English raids. The church has largely gone, its stone taken to build Edinburgh's new tollbooth in the wake of the Reformation. In contrast, the domestic ranges are well preserved. The refectory, dormitory and guesthouse – a series of vaulted halls arranged around a cloister – remained in use for many years as an occasional residence for the island's owners.

There is a chapter house dating from the 13th century, with a warming house above, reached by a staircase from the dormitory; this would once have been the only room to have a fire and must certainly have been much appreciated. Compared to the famous abbeys in the Borders, such as Dryburgh or Melrose, Inchcolm seems architecturally severe. Isolated from the world, it was not intended for display, but as a sanctuary for contemplation and prayer.

Lennoxlove hall

✵ ✵ A late-medieval tower house, with Jacobean and Restoration interiors

Near Haddington, 18 miles E of Edinburgh; private house, open part year

Lennoxlove is truly beautiful. Its large L-plan tower was built by the Maitlands in the early 15th century, probably incorporating older work. The main block was added in the 1620s by John Maitland, Earl of Lauderdale. Later in the century the house was completed by his son, the 1st (and last) Duke of Lauderdale, who ran Scotland as his private fiefdom during the reign of Charles II. More recent changes have largely been cosmetic. Robert Lorimer gave the house an overhaul in 1912 and the 14th Duke of Hamilton brought in Colefax and Fowler when he bought the place in 1946. In 2007 the house re-opened after a lengthy £3-million restoration.

The Great Hall is impressively baronial with bare stone walls, a fine fireplace and heraldic carvings, all courtesy of Lorimer. On the floor above, the Lady's Bower has early plasterwork and a bed that supposedly was slept in by Mary, Queen of Scots, albeit while imprisoned in another house. There is a queasily realistic death-mask of the queen and the silver casket that contained the notorious 'casket letters' linking Mary to the murder of her husband, Lord Darnley. Exhibits on show in the Museum Room include the map and compass used by Rudolf Hess when he parachuted into Scotland in 1941 hoping, quite bizarrely, to negotiate a treaty with the 14th Duke.

Much of the furniture and paintings come from Hamilton Palace, which was demolished in the 1920s. Since the recent restoration, everything looks spick-and-span. Sadly, some of the patina of age has been scrubbed away along with all the scuffs and stains.

Above The Great Hall was refurbished by Robert Lorimer in 1912. He was commissioned by the Hall's then owner, Major William Baird, a descendant of the Blantyres who had lived at Lennoxlove since the early 18th century.

Linlithgow palace

★★★ Impressive ruined remains of a royal palace

At Linlithgow, 15 miles W of Edinburgh; Historic Scotland, open all year

Of all Scotland's former royal palaces, Linlithgow is the most atmospheric. On a misty winter afternoon, its dark vaulted corridors and roofless halls can seem to seethe with spirits from the once-splendid courts of Stuart kings.

The building is more complex than it first appears. Despite its square-cut, monolithic form, it was not the product of a single architectural design, but evolved over a period of some 200 years. In 1425, the royal manor of Linlithgow was destroyed by fire and James I at once ordered its rebuilding on a larger scale. Remarkably, the main façade of this medieval building still remains pretty much unchanged, forming the east front of the present palace. The old entrance, now a gaping archway high above ground, is magnificently ostentatious, with the royal arms carved in relief between the drawbridge slots. James III and James IV added further towers and wings to enclose the courtyard to the building's rear, then in the 1530s, James V moved the entrance to the south and fiddled with the towers for the sake of symmetry. In 1607 the north range collapsed and had to be rebuilt, but by then James VI was also James I of England and the palace was scarcely any longer used. It was pretty much in ruins by 1746, when a force of Cumberland's 'redcoats' camped there overnight. A fire broke out as they departed in the morning and little was done to stop the flames spreading through the empty rooms. Since then, Linlithgow has remained a shell.

The central courtyard has a continental feel, reminiscent of a chateau or *palazzo*, with a hint of English Tudor in James V's south range. The fountain dates from 1538. Tiered like a gothic wedding cake, it has been heavily restored; in keeping with Historic Scotland's conservation policy, there is no attempt to blend the new stonework with the old. Even with most upper floors destroyed, the scale of the palace is breathtaking, The grandest room is the Great Hall, remodelled by James IV in about 1500. A high stone vault adds grandeur to the hall's 'high end', where the king and his circle would have dined. A door in the wall behind leads to a small royal loo.

The hall, chapel and other public rooms are separated from the courtyard by a multi-level labyrinth of corridors and stairs. These form a complex circulation system that was most unusual for the time. On the first floor of the west range, a small room lying at the end of the grand sequence of the King's Apartments has particular charm. With a cosy little fireplace and an oriel window with a view out across the loch, it was probably James V's private chapel or study, providing a welcome refuge from the court and public life.

Above At the heart of the courtyard at Linlithgow is a fountain, created at the behest of James V as a wedding gift for Mary of Guise in 1538. In 1745, when Bonnie Prince Charlie stopped at the palace on his march south, the fountain flowed, it is said, with red wine in his honour. In the 1930s, the fountain was damaged by harsh chemicals used to destroy algae, but recent restoration work has ensured that water can now flow through its sculpted spouts once more.

Newhailes

★★★ A Palladian villa with remarkable original decor

At Mussselburgh, 5 miles E of Edinburgh; National Trust for Scotland, open part year

Newhailes exemplifies the National Trust for Scotland's current conservation policy: 'to do as much as necessary, but as little as possible.' Since the house's acquisition by the Trust in 1997, a fortune has been spent on saving the fabric and contents from terminal decay, and on making what was a very private home suitable for public display. But, refreshingly, it is far from obvious quite how this money has been spent. With flaking paint and chipped chandeliers, the rooms still exude the faded grandeur of benign, upper-class neglect. Newhailes was home to the Dalrymple family for the best part of three centuries, and it still has a lived-in feel.

The house is of great architectural significance. The central block of seven bays was built by the architect James Smith who, along with Sir William Bruce, introduced Palladian design to Scotland in the closing decades of the 17th century. Smith was forced to sell owing to financial difficulties, and so in 1709 the villa and its small estate were acquired by Sir David Dalrymple, the Eton-educated Lord Advocate of Scotland.

Dalrymple added an east wing to provide a home for his substantial library. His son, Sir James, restored the building's symmetry with a matching wing to the west, completed in the 1730s. Since then the whims of fashion have left Newhailes remarkably unscathed, with even the 18th-century suite of dining room, drawing room, bedroom and closet retaining much of its original layout and decor. Rare and fascinating details have survived, including richly decorated plasterwork by Thomas Clayton. In the Chinese Sitting Room real gilded scallop shells are fastened to walls and their form

'... the **whims of fashion** have left Newhailes **remarkably unscathed ...**'

Above The library at Newhailes was built for Sir David Dalrymple in 1718; a portrait by Sir John Baptiste de Medina of Sir David and his son James, c1695, is part of the overmantel. It was James's son – another Sir David – who added to his grandfather's books to create a superb collection of more than 7000 volumes, now in the National Library of Scotland.

recurs throughout the house in the Rococo decor. On other walls, dark faded landscapes and *trompe l'œil* swags and festoons are painted on panelling in a style fashionable in the 1730s.

Sir David Dalrymple's library is the largest and grandest room by far. Dr Johnson is said to have described it as 'the most learned drawing room in Europe', not on account of the company he met there, but for the books he found on its shelves. Sadly, the room has suffered a tragic loss and its shelves are now bare. In 1971, on the death of Sir Mark Dalrymple, some 7000 volumes were passed to the National Library of Scotland in lieu of death duties. The National Trust for Scotland still hopes that this unique collection from the Scottish Enlightenment may be restored to its proper home, and thus bring Newhailes truly back to life.

Glasgow & the West

the west

Culzean Castle

Blairquhan

★ A Regency mansion in English-Tudor style

Near Straiton, 13 miles S of Ayr; private house, open part year

Blairquhan is a handsome house, dressed up with the elegance of a Regency dandy. Built in the 1820s, it was an early work of William Burn, an architect who would help to re-define the style of Britain's country houses. The look he pursued for Blairquhan is English-Tudor, a highly fashionable style before the more exuberant Scots Baronial caught on.

Burn's client was Sir David Hunter Blair, the scion of a well-respected Ayrshire family, who had purchased the estate some twenty years before. A large and rather splendid castle had to be demolished to make way for his new bespoke mansion. Inside, the main rooms all open off a spectacular 60-foot-high saloon, top-lit and with galleries cantilevered out at first-floor level. Symmetry is obsessively observed, with twenty-two matching doors, many of them false, and twin fireplaces just yards apart. In an age of strict formality a gentleman's house, just like his necktie, had to look balanced. The double doors lead through to a double-flighted stair.

Today, Blairquhan is still in the same family. The house is lovingly maintained, but the days when there were eighteen servants have long gone, and toys lie scattered on the floors. Portraits, furniture and family mementoes are more intriguing than memorable. In a courtyard to the rear, ornate stonework from the old castle is included in the walls. A set of heads, with wonderfully animated faces, are probably caricatures of their anonymous sculptor's 16th-century workmates.

Burns' cottage

★ The cottage where Robert Burns was born

At Alloway, 2 miles S of Ayr; museum, open all year

It is not only Scots who are devoted to the memory of Robert Burns. A steady stream of devotees descend on Alloway, and on the 250th anniversary of his birth, coming up in January 2009, pilgrims are expected to come from every corner of the world to admire the Brig o'Doon, the Burns Monument, the Auld Kirk and even the 'Tam o'Shanter Experience'.

The poet's actual birthplace is a quaint thatched cottage that looks rather out of kilter with its neighbours in the town's high street. It was built in 1757 by Robert's father William, a self-educated gardener who planned to establish his own business on the small plot of land. The project failed and the family moved on in 1766, when Robert was only seven. By the time of his death, thirty years later, the cottage was an alehouse, where the world's first Burns Supper was held in 1801. In 1881 it was acquired by the Burns Monument Trustees and has been preserved ever since as a shrine.

The building has been much extended since the 18th century, when the whole family lived and slept in just one room. It is restored to immaculate condition, and still contains the original box-bed in which Robert was born. Although all other furnishings have been imported, the room looks most convincing and is said to move some visitors to tears. There is a museum of memorabilia next door.

Robert Burns
1759–96

Robert Burns, Scotland's best-known and arguably greatest poet, shot to fame in 1786 with the publication of his first collection, *Poems, Chiefly in the Scottish Dialect*. He was hailed as 'the ploughman poet' and admired for what was felt to be a natural, untutored genius for encapsulating commonly shared emotions and experience. He remains popular worldwide.

Culzean castle

★★★ A theatrical castle designed by Robert Adam

12 miles SW of Ayr; National Trust for Scotland, open part year

Culzean Castle is a product of a favourite 18th-century topic for debate: the clash between sense and sensibility, between reason and romance. In 1775, David Kennedy became the 10th Earl of Cassillis and, along with large estates, he inherited a tower house that the Kennedys had held since the dawn of time – or, to be more prosaic, for around 400 years. Its position on a cliff-top, high above a rocky shore, was spectacular. It was a building that embodied the historic essence of the clan, but for a sophisticated British nobleman of the late 18th century, it was embarrassingly out of date.

The 9th Earl had made some efforts to remodel it, but it was, like all such ancient towers, damp and dark, with an awkward labyrinth of rooms and far too many stairs. Even so, the new Earl found it quite unthinkable to tear it down. Instead, he turned to Robert Adam – no longer quite the darling of the age, but still possessed of an ambitiously inventive mind – to transform his decrepit old monument into a desirable seat.

Adam gave the Earl exactly what he wanted – a romantic castle with battlements and towers that included the ancestral stronghold in its core, yet had classical façades and stylish

Above left The Round Drawing Room was left unfinished by Adam and the plasterwork was completed in the Regency period by the 12th Earl. The carpet is a copy of the original – now being conserved – made in 1983 by a local Irvine firm.
Above right The Blue Drawing room is the most complete Adam room at Culzean; the plasterwork was finished before his death in 1792. The blue silk wall coverings are part of the National Trust's reinstatement of the original colour scheme.

modern rooms. It was a dream-house for the Age of Reason, but it would take more than twenty years to finish, thanks to extravagant additions to the original design. In 1790 the entire centre section of the north front had to be removed to install the oval staircase. But far from worrying about the budget, the Earl urged Adam on in 'his romantic genius'. He died in December 1792, nine months after Adam, heavily in debt, with the house still unfinished.

Unequivocally, it was worth the effort. The castle looks sensational and there is much to be seen. A thousand weapons in the entrance hall (acquired by the 13th Earl as a job lot from the Tower of London) are the only hint of castle-like character allowed indoors. The oval staircase is superbly elegant, as is the Round Drawing Room

in a tower overlooking the open sea. The plasterwork is beautifully executed and painted, and it takes an expert eye to distinguish between Robert Adam's original creations, Regency variations on his designs and late-Victorian Adam-style revivals in papier mâché. The paintings and furniture are all exquisite.

Culzean has been through many changes over the years, and although in some old houses this results in a fascinating palimpsest of overlapping layers, at Culzean the result is more confused. It is seldom clear whether one is looking at an original Adam design or some later variation. But does it matter? This really is a splendid house, even if some of the reality does not quite succeed in living up to the castle's promise of romance.

Dean castle

★★ A restored medieval keep and palace

At Kilmarnock, 12 miles NE of Ayr; museum, open all year for tours only

With its massive keep, separate 'palace' range, timber-framed wall-head walk and assorted other buildings, Dean Castle looks like a perfect medieval castle. Too perfect – no ancient building could remain so completely unaltered through the years. There has clearly been a great deal of first-class creative reconstruction, so cleverly accomplished that it is now hard to distinguish old from new.

The Boyds, who began the castle in the 14th century, were a family who played for high stakes in a chaotic age. In the 1460s, Robert, the first Lord Boyd, became Governor of the Realm during the minority of James III, holding the young king as a virtual prisoner in Edinburgh. The 'palace' range that he added to the castle is a statement of his confidence, but shortly afterwards his faction was overthrown and he fled to England under sentence of death.

For the next three centuries of civil and religious disputes, the family continued to play with fire until William Boyd, the 4th Earl of Kilmarnock, was captured at Culloden and executed. By then, the castle was a ruin, having been accidentally incinerated in 1735.

In 1905 the crumbling buildings were acquired by Lord Howard de Walden, who spent the next thirty years on their painstaking restoration. The high, vaulted hall in the medieval keep looks magnificently primitive, although the bare stonework is a product of Edwardian ideas of how a castle should appear. In the 'palace' the fabulous 16th-century plaster ceiling, although brought in from elsewhere, provides a more convincing take on Renaissance Scots decor. Other buildings within the walled courtyard were built from scratch with reclaimed stone.

Lord Howard used the castle as his private museum and his remarkable collections remain. The Great Hall contains medieval weaponry and armour, all of first-rate quality, with a pair of early Flemish tapestries hanging on the walls. There is an even finer tapestry in the chamber above – an altar-piece by the late-15th century 'Master of Gudule.'

Dumfries house

☆ ☆ ☆   A fine Adam house with a unique collection of original furniture

Near Cumnock, 12 mile S of Kilmarnock; private house, expected to open part year

In the summer of 2007 the fate of Dumfries House hung in the balance. It looked almost certain that the Adam mansion, along with its estate, would be sold to some anonymous global billionaire and its extraordinary contents dispersed at auction. Then, at the eleventh hour, Prince Charles stepped in, brokering a deal worth £45 million that saved the entire ensemble for the nation. Conservationists rejoiced as royalty snipped through the tangle of red tape that surrounds grant-aided projects. The house is now in the care of the Great Steward's Dumfries House Trust, the 'Great Steward of Scotland' being one of Prince Charles's titles.

Externally, the building has a conventional Palladian face. Built in the 1750s for the 5th Earl of Dumfries, it was one of the first country house commissions for the Adam brothers following their father William's death, and Robert had not yet been inspired by his Grand Tour of Europe's classical remains.

The main reception rooms and state bedrooms have ornate plasterwork by Thomas

Right Above the fireplace in the North Drawing Room is a *trompe l'œil* grisaille painting of three charming putti – one is busy painting while the other two look on.

'Some **fifty pieces**
[by Chippendale] ...
remain *in situ.*'

Above When Dumfries House was extended at the end of the 19th century, by Arts-and-Crafts architect Robert Weir Schultz, the cedar-panelled Tapestry Room was created to display Gobelins tapestries given to the 2nd Earl of Stair by Louis XIV. The Earl of Stair, uncle of the 5th Earl of Dumfries who built the house, was ambassador to France in the early 1700s.

Clayton, with dense swags of foliage so finely moulded they appear as if carved from wood. On the first floor, the decor is devoid of such extravagance, but the architectural design is more adventurous. The bedrooms open off a top-lit central gallery that runs the full width of the house between two sets of stairs.

The cost of the house, according to surviving bills, was nearly £8,000, but this sum did not, of course, include the furnishings. For these, the Earl turned to the most fashionable interior designer of the day, Thomas Chippendale. Some fifty pieces – from beds and bookcases to mirrors and pole-screens – were designed for specific rooms and made in Chippendale's own workshop. Other pieces, plainer and less

valuable but of almost equal interest and rarity, were acquired in Edinburgh from Alexander Peter and other top Scottish cabinet-makers. All still remain *in situ*.

When the house passed by marriage to the Marquesses of Bute, it became a secondary residence that was rarely used. In the 1890s the 3rd Marquess took time out from his project at Mount Stuart (see page 143) to enlarge the pavilion wings, one of which was specifically designed to house a set of Gobelins tapestries. Apart from this, Dumfries House has slumbered through the years, well-maintained but scarcely changed from the day it was first built. Now it is about to be awoken and, for the first time in its history, opened up to public view.

Holmwood house

Netherlee Road, Glasgow; National Trust for Scotland, open part year

After Charles Rennie Mackintosh, Alexander 'Greek' Thomson is Glasgow's most famous architect. Born half a century before Mackintosh, he was, arguably, as original. He is best known for his extraordinary churches, but he was also responsible for a variety of other works. Holmwood is the finest of several villas that he built for wealthy clients during Glasgow's boom years of manufacture and trade.

Completed in 1858 for the owner of a local paper-mill, Holmwood is visually astounding. As a building it bridges the divide between classical and picturesque, with a hint of proto-modernism stirred into the mix. In a later generation, Frank Lloyd Wright would crib certain of its elements for his 'Prairie' houses.

The architecture is in line with the Greek-Revival style that had earlier made Edinburgh the so-called 'Athens of the North', but Playfair or Hamilton would have been bewildered by Holmwood's lack of symmetry and wilful oddity of form. Thomson had never been to Greece or Rome – his vision of antiquity derived from prints and pattern-books, unrestrained by actuality, and his imagination thrived on epic poetry, masonic rituals and bible tales. Looking for a source from which a new, spiritually pure architecture could derive, he brought together Mycenae, Jerusalem and Thebes to achieve effects that are inspiring – but strange.

The interior is perhaps even odder than the exterior. As an architect of fanatical conviction (a trait he shared with Mackintosh), Thomson saw his houses not as shells but as integrated works of art, with decor, furniture and fabrics all finished to his own designs. Sadly, Holmwood's

Left Holmwood was owned by nuns before it was acquired by the National Trust, and the dining room was used as a chapel. The Sisters felt that the subject matter of the frieze running round the room was inappropriate, so papered over it. Restoration has revealed the paintings beneath. **Below** Alexander Thomson suggested to his client, James Couper, that the round bay window in the parlour was 'a fitting spot' for the ladies of Holmwood to set up their work tables.

GLASGOW

furniture was long ago dispersed, but the decor is now undergoing painstaking restoration by the National Trust for Scotland.

In the dining room, a frieze illustrating scenes from Homer's Iliad has been exposed, reviving the splendour of the villa's grandest room. Throughout the house, windows of unique design pushed Victorian techniques of glass-production to the limits. In the dining room, enormous plate-glass sheets are recessed behind free-standing columns to give the impression of an open portico. In the parlour, panes curve audaciously around three quarters of a circle that is completed in the plasterwork above. In the stair-hall, light pours down from a cupola to seep along sombre corridors, with faded ochre paint flaking from their walls.

Most woodwork is left bare, with doors of pine adorned with intricate fretwork panels of mahogany. Such details were cut by machinery, for unlike later Arts-and-Crafts revivalists, Thomson was enthusiastic about new technologies. This allowed some useful savings and, for all its fantastical elaborations, Holmwood cost just £3,600, a very modest sum for a house of such apparent grandeur. Masquerading as a dream palace, it is actually a bourgeois home of entirely practical design.

Pollok house

★★ A Georgian house with neo-Georgian interiors and some splendid art

Pollokshaws Road, Glasgow; National Trust for Scotland, open all year

Dating from the late 1740s, Pollok House was probably designed by Glasgow architect Allan Dreghorn, working in the style that William Adam had made almost *de rigeur* for Scottish lairds. A series of castles on the site had been home to the Maxwell family since the 13th century. Their descendants still maintain a flat within the house.

In the 1890s and early 1900s, the building was enlarged and modernized by Robert Rowand Anderson for Sir John Maxwell, an enthusiastic conservationist who became a co-founder of the Trust in 1931. Although now managed by the Trust, the house was gifted to the City of Glasgow by Sir John's daughter, Anne, in 1966. Pollok's extensive grounds were then selected as a suitable home for the world-famous Burrell Collection of art, which had been given to the City of Glasgow in 1944.

The Edwardian reconstruction was unusually respectful of the Georgian house. Elaborate plasterwork by Thomas Clayton was retained in the reception rooms and new, single-storey wings were built in Palladian style. The entrance incorporates the time-worn pediment and columns of the original front door, yet leads into a hall as Edwardian as the foyer of a London club, with a double staircase and huge electric lantern. The library, also from the 1900s, is equally theatrical, divided into three compartments by arches sprung from paired Ionic columns. Furniture, mostly neo-Georgian, is sparse and formally arranged. A 'lived-in' feel has been attempted in one of the bedrooms, with clothes on the sofa and a table set for breakfast.

The chief interest of Pollok House is in the paintings that hang on the walls of every room. Acquired largely by Sir William Maxwell in the mid-19th century, they range from Renaissance portraits to works by William Blake, and include one of Britain's most significant collections of Spanish art. Alongside the cold, cruel faces of in-bred Habsburg princes there is a radiant El Greco, *Lady in a Fur Wrap*, and a pair of small but powerful Goyas satirizing politics and religion in the guise of children's games.

The Tenement house

★★☆ An original tenement flat, preserved in an Edwardian time-warp

Buccleuch Street, Glasgow; National Trust for Scotland, open part year

Like a crime-scene sealed off for forensic study, the Tenement House is a slice of social history in an inner-city flat. The red sandstone tenements of Buccleuch Street, built in 1892, were at the speculative limit of the city's westward sprawl at the time. They were aimed at what were then the pillars of society: the respectable, hard working, lower middle class.

From 1911 until 1965, No 145 was home to Miss Agnes Toward, who lived there first with her mother, then in later years, alone. Miss Toward was a shorthand typist who remained with the same firm all her working life. She was a self-reliant woman, frugal in her habits, and made few changes to her home, which took on an increasingly old-fashioned character as the century progressed. By good fortune the next owner, who acquired the flat complete with all its contents after Miss Toward's death, was so entranced by this unique Edwardian survival that she, too, kept the place pretty much unchanged. She sold the flat to the National Trust for Scotland in 1982.

The flat, or 'house' as homes in Glasgow tenements are known, has a spacious hall and four rooms: a parlour, kitchen, bedroom and bathroom. Furnished with Miss Toward's own possessions and with the original decor restored, it has more to say about the living in the early 20th century than a library of books. The parlour ('kept for best' and with a piano), the closet beds, the coal-bunker in the kitchen – all hark back to a time that was slower, simpler and more constrained than ours.

Yet when the Towards first arrived, the tenement must have seemed luxurious. The bathroom with its flushing lavatory and the boiler for hot water were prizes of modernity that such a family would not have dreamt of owning just a generation before. There are mementos of Miss Toward in every room; photographs and postcards, perfume bottles, clothes, crockery and knick-knacks. Just occasionally a detail jars. The proud old lady's spirit must be mortified that her chamber-pot is openly displayed. It would have been put away when visitors called by.

Left The kitchen of the Tenement House is dominated by the black coal-fired range which was used for cooking. The fire also heated water in a boiler behind the range, and this was stored in a hot-water tank in a small cupboard to the right of the range. It was piped to the kitchen sink, in front of the window, and to the bathroom next door. **Below** In one corner of the parlour a door leads into a bed closet, a useful way of providing extra sleeping quarters in a small flat. Such built-in beds were banned after 1900 for health reasons.

'...a slice of social history ...'

The Hill house

★★★★☆ The Arts-and-Crafts masterpiece of Charles Rennie Mackintosh

At Helensburgh, 8 miles NW of Dumbarton; National Trust for Scotland, open part year

Charles Rennie Mackintosh's stellar reputation as a pioneer of modern architecture rests on a very small body of completed works. Despite the early admiration for his style among the European avant-garde, he remained an outsider in his native land and The Hill House – built in 1902 for the Glasgow publisher Walter Blackie – was one of only two commissions he received to design private homes from scratch. The project allowed Mackintosh considerable creative freedom. Today, the house remains a remarkably complete ensemble, giving us a true measure of its creator's talent.

The site is superb, facing south across the Firth of Clyde from the high ridge above Helensburgh, in an enclave of exclusive villas. In addition to designing the building itself, Mackintosh was involved in every detail of interior decor, as well as many of the furnishings, always working closely with his wife, the talented Margaret Macdonald. Most of the contents still remain in place, while other long-lost pieces have been reinstated and the original colour schemes have been restored since ownership passed to the National Trust for Scotland.

Charles Rennie Mackintosh
1868–1928

Charles Rennie Mackintosh was born in Glasgow into a family of modest means. He was apprenticed to a local architect at the age of 16, and in 1889 he joined Honeyman and Keppie, the firm with whom he remained throughout his working life.

The outstanding building of his early career was Glasgow's School of Art, which brought him international recognition. The Willow Tearooms in Glasgow are a fine example of his interior design, undertaken in collaboration with his wife, Margaret Macdonald. But Mackintosh also gained a reputation for being 'difficult'. After Hill House he received few commissions and he retired from practice before the First World War. The couple later moved to the South of France, where he lived as an artist until his death.

Mackintosh's reputation grew as the 20th century progressed. His 'House for an Art Lover', designed in 1901, was finally built in Glasgow in the 1990s, a tribute to his talent and lasting influence.

'... a remarkably **complete ensemble** ... a true measure of its **creator's talent.'**

Above A long window bay in the drawing room of The Hill House looks out over a south-facing terrace. The rose motif that decorates the walls and upholstery of the room was intended to bring elements from the garden into the house. The cube table is made of ebonized wood, decorated with tiny inlaid squares of mother-of-pearl.

When the house was completed, Mackintosh remarked: 'It is not an Italian Villa, an English Mansion House, a Swiss Chalet, or a Scotch Castle. It is a Dwelling House.' This is true, but is somewhat disingenuous. Unlike most architecture of Mackintosh's day, The Hill House has no fancy-dress pretence, but the building's outer form shows a clear understanding and appreciation of place and tradition. An angle-tower rises to a little turret with a pointy roof, chimney-stacks stand proud against the sky, wings thrust out with force, while throughout the design the lack of formal symmetry is balanced with geometric grace. In essence, the Scottish tower house has been refined and given an entirely modern face. The details are superb, and the more you look the more you see. The interplay between light and shade is ever-changing. From very first sight, The Hill House is bewitching.

The tower house theme does not continue indoors. If influences are at work at all, they might be Japanese mixed with English Arts and Crafts, but the style is really all down to Mackintosh himself. The long dark hallway seems to recall a forest, with timber verticals supporting a latticework of beams and dappled light filtering through small glass panels to mimic the effect of leaves. What better introduction to the home of a publisher of fairy tales?

Leaving the magical domain of the hall, the visitor enters the bright, cream-painted, south-facing drawing room. Here, the sun streams in through the windows, illuminating stencilled roses on the walls. Like an enchanted garden, this is a space for cultivated souls to take their ease.

Upstairs in the main bedroom, the bed is recessed in a vaulted alcove. A pair of embroidered angels – faithful copies of the original hangings created by Margaret Macdonald for the room – stand guard over the sleeper's head. Many houses in Scotland speak of ancestry and power, but The Hill House explores the mind and soul.

In all the main rooms (with the exception of the dining room, of which more below), furniture and decor are intrinsic to the scheme. There are a number of Mackintosh's signature chairs, looking elegant but uncomfortable. The finest individual piece (on show only between April and July) is Mrs Blackie's writing desk, for which the Trust and Glasgow City Council paid just under £1 million at auction in 2002. Built of ebonized wood inlaid with mother-of-pearl and ivory, it opens up in the

Below In the main hall, Mackintosh used panels of dark-stained pine on the walls, with an abstract frieze. In addition to the window, light comes from the small glass panels in the main door and from large rectangular pendant lights, decorated with stylized representations of the seedheads of honesty.

'A pair of embroidered angels ...
stand guard over the sleeper's head.'

Above The main bedroom is L-shaped and the carved bed stands hidden in its own cosy, arched alcove. The space is lit by a small window, set in its own curved recess. Shutters pierced with six small rose-pink panes of glass can be closed over the window at night. More pink is found in the stylized rose-and-trellis pattern stencilled on the walls.

form of a kimono. Like the house itself, the desk is an exquisite masterpiece masquerading as an object of utility. Above the drawing room fireplace there is an interesting gesso panel, again by Margaret, portraying the tale of Sleeping Beauty in a style reminiscent of the Viennese Secessionists.

The dining room comes as something of a surprise. The Blackies owned some antique furniture, which they insisted on retaining. Although the originals have gone, the Trust has, quite properly, reinstated the room in a style true to the Blackies' time there, with some respectable Georgian pieces. It must be said that they look utterly absurd. It is not merely that such furniture clashes with Mackintosh's decor for the room – it is screamingly unsuited to the house. Some might say that the Blackies should have had more respect for the artistic integrity of the house, but this was, after all, their home. A more accommodating architect, such as a Lorimer or Lutyens, might have eased the confrontation between traditional and modern, but for Mackintosh there could be no compromise.

Kelburn castle

★★ A medieval house with Georgian and Victorian wings

17 miles SW of Paisley; private house, open by arrangement

Parts of Kelburn Castle may date back to the 12th century, when the Boyle family were newly settled in the area. They acquired considerable wealth, enabling John Boyle, in 1581, to encase his antiquated keep within a substantial, fashionably elaborate tower house in castellated style. By 1700 this, in turn, was seen as out of date and so David Boyle – soon to become Earl of Glasgow – built on a brand new wing. Externally plain, the new wing contained rooms of opulent Baroque decor. Another wing was added in the 1870s by the 6th Earl, who was also responsible for spending most of the family's considerable fortune on church-building and other 'good works'.

Since then, Kelburn has endured a slow, genteel decline, and the sense of slightly threadbare, eccentric aristocracy adds greatly to the castle's character. After centuries of

occupation as a home, the place is full of surprises. There is a particularly fine Raeburn portrait in the dining room and a stuffed albatross half way up the stairs. The drawing room is magnificent – a double-cube room with Corinthian pilasters and a richly decorated frieze of carved wood painted to resemble plaster. The huge, multi-paned sash windows would have been a startling innovation when they were installed in 1700.

The future of the castle today looks secure, thanks to the sale of building plots on the estate. As plans are drawn up for renovation work, the tower has been painted with cartoon-style murals by a group of Brazilian graffiti artists under the direction of the Earl's young heir, Viscount Kelburn. Few visitors over the age of thirty will approve, but it will all come off when the harling is replaced.

Newark castle

⭐ An historic tower house overlooking the River Clyde

At Port Glasgow, 4 miles E of Greenock; Historic Scotland, open part year

For many years, Newark Castle lay little noticed and neglected, overshadowed by the gantries of Port Glasgow's shipyards. At one point in the 19th century, a dealer in exotic animals kept bears and panthers in the cellars, and joiners and rope-makers lived in the once-palatial rooms above. Now, with the lower reaches of the Clyde striving towards a post-industrial revival, the castle has regained some measure of its former splendour.

The oldest parts – the gatehouse and a sturdy, square-built tower – were constructed in the 1480s by George Maxwell, a courtier of James IV. The King himself stayed there in 1495 at the outset of a naval expedition to suppress the Lordship of the Isles. Around a century later, Patrick Maxwell – a courtier renowned both for his refinement and his brutality – incorporated these remnants of the original defensive castle into the magnificent building that we see today. Despite murdering several of his neighbours and maltreating his wife, Patrick escaped justice thanks to his friendship with James VI.

The building's long decline began in 1668 when its grounds were sold to allow the development of a new sea-port for Glasgow. But never having fallen completely into ruin, nor been fashionably 'improved', the house has retained much of its integrity. In the ground-floor kitchen, the original water inlet and waste chute remain in place. There is a beautifully carved fireplace in the first-floor hall, and a small sink beside the door where guests could wash their hands before they dined. The most remarkable survival is a bedchamber which still has painted decoration on its beams, a closed-off privy in the wall and a panelled closet for a bed.

New Lanark

★★★★ An early industrial centre built with humanitarian ideals

Near Lanark, 12 miles SE of Motherwell; museum, open all year

New Lanark is Britain's best-preserved industrial community from the early 1800s, with mills, housing, schools and other structures barely changed and immaculately restored. Its significance is not merely architectural: in the early years, the mill and it surrounding village comprised a Utopian experiment – an attempt to marry capitalist enterprise with the principles of socialism. New Lanark was intended as a model society. Such ideals were not universal – the 'dark satanic mills' described by William Blake became the industrial norm – but the New Lanark experiment was repeated elsewhere in Britain, and it continues to inspire today.

It was the power of the river surging through a narrow channel that first attracted David Dale and his partner Robert Arkwright to this wooded gorge in 1785. The complex they constructed below the waterfalls of Cora Lynn became Scotland's largest manufacturing enterprise, with a workforce of more than 1300, a third of them children. By the standards of the time, conditions were humane, but New Lanark's golden age did not begin until after 1800, when Dale sold out to his son-in-law, the visionary Robert Owen (Arkwright had already left the scene).

Over the next quarter of a century, Robert Owen constructed houses and facilities for his workers, in addition to the mills they worked in. He increasingly assumed the role of benevolent dictator, launching what he would immodestly describe as 'the most important experiment for the happiness of the human race'. Child labour was phased out and education was provided from infancy to adulthood. These worthy endeavours were accompanied by a more worrying level of surveillance and control. Anti-social behaviour, drunkenness and failure to meet production targets all attracted penalties. Community-appointed 'watchmen' even conducted weekly checks on the cleanliness of homes.

By the time Owen left New Lanark in 1825 – to found another community in Indiana, USA – the population of his Scottish utopia had grown to 2300. But as the 19th century progressed, New Lanark passed from the attention of the wider world. The mills eventually closed in 1968 and soon just 80 inhabitants remained. For a while, demolition seemed the only option.

Revival began in 1974, when a Conservation Trust was established. In 2001, New Lanark received the ultimate accolade of recognition by UNESCO as a World Heritage Site. The population is now above 200, with tourism replacing industry as its raison d'être.

Of the mills themselves – all beautifully restored – one is a hotel and others contain offices, craft shops and cafes. Mill Number 3 has working looms and original machinery. The main visitor centre is in Owen's Institution for the Formation of Character, the adult-education centre where baths were provided before lectures. The School for Children contains a re-created classroom. There is also the village shop, established by Owen on cooperative lines.

Most of the tenements are occupied as homes and although one has been preserved 'as found', it is deemed too cramped for visitors. Instead, there are two re-creations on offer, one a home from the 1930s and the other, from the early years, a sparsely furnished room for a family of six – hardly a vision of the New Jerusalem, but a measure of how bad the slums were elsewhere. Owen's own home is on show, with rooms furnished in a generic late-Georgian style. While palatial in comparison to the housing of his workers, it is a home that would be considered spartan by any chief executive in industry today.

As an experience, New Lanark is more than the sum of its individual parts. The soul-stirring mix of architecture, history, landscape and dreams gives the place star quality.

... the complex ... became Scotland's **largest manufacturing** enterprise.'

The Highlands

Eilean Donan Castle

The Highlands & Islands

Arnol blackhouse

★ A traditional Hebridean dwelling of simple construction

11 miles NW of Stornoway, Isle of Lewis; Historic Scotland, open all year

Arnol Blackhouse is unique. It is the only building of its type to have been preserved in original condition, complete with furniture and personal possessions, as though frozen in a time-warp on the day it was abandoned. Blackhouses were once common throughout the Highlands and they survived in the Western Isles later than elsewhere. Each island developed its own style – those on Lewis were long and narrow. They resemble Norse houses of a thousand years before and their ruins can be seen in every yard behind the drab but comfortable bungalows of modern Arnol.

'Blackhouses ... resemble Norse houses of a thousand years before ...'

Right At the heart of the blackhouse living room is a central hearth, the *cagailt*, fuelled by peat. Traditionally, there was no chimney to allow smoke from the fire to escape; the only openings in the roof were covered with thin animal skins that let in light and kept in smoke. The idea was that the smoke would impregnate the thatch with peaty soot, then each year this was removed and used as a fertilizer on the fields.

Despite its almost prehistoric appearance, with window-less walls of rubble and a thatch roof weighted down with stones, this blackhouse was built in around 1880 and only finally abandoned in 1966. At the centre of the living-room, a peat fire smoulders. In the absence of a chimney, the smoke forms a faint, sweet-smelling haze that rises to seep slowly through the roof. A huge kettle hangs from the rafter over the fire. This was where the family cooked and ate their meals. After dark it was where they worked, read and talked. There is a box-bed in a corner,

with two further beds in a small room beyond. The furniture is simple, consisting of dressers, a table and a settle ranged against the walls. Wallpaper was nailed to the ceiling beams in an attempt at fashionable decor, but this has since been removed.

Although a careful reconstruction, the house is clearly not presented exactly as it was lived in. A family of ten of twelve would have occupied this cramped space, with cattle in the byre under the same roof (the dung was carried away through the front door). The house celebrates a vanished culture and, as in Gaelic folk-songs, there is more than a hint of dewy-eyed nostalgia.

Brodick castle

★ ★ ★ The splendid Scots-Baronial home of an ambitious Duke

On the Isle of Arran, 14 miles W of Ardrossan; National Trust for Scotland, open part year

Brodick Castle bristles with towers, battlements and turrets, a romantic extravaganza standing majestically above Brodick Bay, with the mountain of Goatfell as a backdrop. The castle's history is rich in tales of nobility and bloodshed dating back into the 13th century.

After repeated battering and rebuilding over the course of feuds and wars, Brodick was granted in 1503 to James Hamilton, a cousin of King James IV. Hamilton's descendants would become one of Scotland's most influential families, first as Earls of Arran then, from 1643, as the Dukes of Hamilton. As Earls they even contended for the throne, lurching between royal favour and disgrace, with bouts of insanity between. As Dukes they were disaster-prone: one died on the scaffold, his successor on the battlefield, leaving debts and no male heir.

The castle was briefly requisitioned and enlarged as a garrison for Oliver Cromwell's army. It was only on account of the second Duke's niece, Duchess Anne (she held the title under her own right), that the castle was returned and the family survived. They would recover to prosper mightily in later years from coal-mines on their Lanarkshire estates and marriages to heiress wives.

It was the 10th Duke who created the castle we see today. Known behind his back as 'Il Magnifico', he was an admirer of Napoleon and nurtured a dynastic

'[The] great tower is a **masterpiece, blending seamlessly** with the **older parts** that it adjoins'

dream of reviving the family's old claim to the Stuart throne. In 1810, aged 47, he married the 24-year-old daughter of William Beckford, an eccentric millionaire whose fantastical treasure-house at Fonthill Abbey was a wonder of the age. In due course a son was born, who in 1843 was married off to Princess Mary of Baden, the daughter of a Habsburg Grand Duke and great-niece of the Empress Josephine. 'Il Magnifico' had already rebuilt his main ducal seat, Hamilton Palace, on a suitably stupendous scale. So now, at the age of 81, he decided that Brodick should become a shooting lodge fit for an emperor of Scotland.

The architect was James Gillespie Graham who managed to nearly triple the size of the castle with a skill that deceives the eye. His great tower is a masterpiece, blending seamlessly with the older parts that it adjoins. The transition between periods is even harder to spot inside, where rooms were decorated in a Jacobean style with ornate Scots-Renaissance ceilings.

Neither Fonthill nor Hamilton Palace have survived, but at least some of their treasures can still be seen at Brodick. The pictures include works by Turner, Gainsborough, Nasmyth and other fine British artists, along with some small but luminous Old Masters. Both Beckford and the Duke were inveterate collectors who had the wealth to outbid any rival. The furniture, porcelain and silver are equally impressive, if at times verging on vulgar – both men had a tendency towards high-camp bad taste. Among the most precious objects on display are a pair of Chinese *famille rose* tureens modelled in the form of geese. Now highly valued, in the past they were reputedly put to use by younger members of the family as goal-posts in games of indoor football.

Castle of Mey

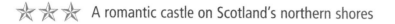 A romantic castle on Scotland's northern shores

Near Mey, 12 miles E of Thurso; private house, open part year

It is easy to see why the Queen Mother was so fond of the Castle of Mey. The old house stands above a wild shore, with scarcely another building to be seen. Towers and turrets form an entrancing silhouette. A garden blooms behind its high walls. Remote and beautiful, the place is a countrywoman's idyll – a private little kingdom by the sea.

Built in the 1560s by George Sinclair, the 4th Earl of Caithness, the castle is a traditional Scots tower house, with a central block of grand apartments flanked diagonally by sturdy towers. The Sinclairs retained ownership until the 1880s, occasionally making alterations, but by the time the

Above The drawing room is furnished very much as it was during the Queen Mother's time. She first saw the castle in 1952 when staying with friends at nearby Dunnet Head, shortly after her husband's death, and bought it the same year. The Queen Mother changed the name from Barrogill Castle back to the original Castle of Mey.

Queen Mother bought the place in 1952 it was in a sorry state, having served as a military billet during World War II. Restoration took three years, after which she holidayed there every August and October until 2001. It is now owned by a trust, with Prince Charles as president (he also stays there, briefly, every year). It is preserved exactly as it was, as though in readiness for his grandmother to arrive.

Both 'upstairs' and 'downstairs' are on show. The entrance is theatrical – a miniature imperial staircase, designed by William Burn in 1819, leads to an outrageously flamboyant jardinière on the landing. The Queen Mother's taste was highly individual and house guests often added to the decor with their own eclectic souvenirs. There is a woolly stag's head hanging on the

library wall and a tartan Nessie perched above a tapestry in the drawing room. The tapestry itself is a magnificent example of 16th-century Flemish craftsmanship and, like most of the castle furnishings, it was personally chosen rather than inherited. Pictures include many works by members of the Royal Family. Guest bedrooms, reached up narrow spiral stairs, are small and were notoriously cold. The dining room, by contrast, is distinctly regal, with trophies and fine silver on display.

Next to the dining room is a butler's pantry, a throw-back to the 1950s with Formica units and an ancient fridge. The kitchen remains equally unmodernized. Frozen in a time-warp, the Castle of Mey is remarkably revealing of its former owner's life and personality.

Cawdor castle

★★★★ A medieval castle steeped in legend

At Cawdor, 5 miles S of Nairn; private house, open part year

Thanks to *Macbeth*, the name Cawdor Castle alone conjures up images of witches and dark deeds. The actual castle fully lives up to this promise, with a working drawbridge and a medieval tower capped by battlements and turrets. In keeping with the setting, there is a history richly spiced with legends of kidnapped heirs, murders, conspiracies and feuds.

Any actual link with the real Macbeth is easily dismissed, since the king died in 1097 and Cawdor was not built until the 14th century. Perhaps Shakespeare simply liked the name, with its ill-omened echo of a raven's call. In any case, the castle has its own foundation myth – a story involving a dream, a donkey and a bag of gold that is best told over a dram or two of malt. The tree that features at the story's climax (it was growing where the dreamer had to build) really does exist. In the dark, vaulted guard-room of the tower, a gnarled trunk sprouts from the floor, its upper branches shackled to an iron ring. Scientific tests have established that it is a holly tree that perished, no doubt from lack of light, in around the year 1372. No trace of the donkey has been found.

Above Legend has it that a Thane of Cawdor was told in a dream to send a donkey into the woods. Wherever the donkey stopped to rest was where the Thane was meant to build his castle. The 'thorn tree', long-dead but still standing in the tower guard-room, is reputedly the very tree where the donkey stopped.

The guard-room with its mythic tree has scarcely changed since medieval times. Next to it is a small cell, discovered in 1979 within the thickness of the wall. Equipped with a privy and a vent, it was entered through a trapdoor from above and may have been designed to provide a secret refuge if the castle was ever stormed. Defence was certainly a priority in the castle's early days and in 1454 the 6th Thane was granted a licence to fortify the tower. The castle then remained little altered for the next 200 years, with the Thane in his tower and his household in now-vanished buildings ranged around the court below.

The present family arrived at Cawdor, as cuckoos in the nest, in the early 16th century. The 8th Thane had died young, leaving an infant daughter as his heir. Now a valuable prize, young Muriel was swiftly kidnapped by a kinsman, the greedily ambitious Earl of Argyll. He raised her like a pet at Inveraray until, at the age of twelve, she agreed to wed his younger son. Some years later, to escape a feud with the Macleans, the couple took up residence in Cawdor, killing off some cousins who by then claimed the castle as their own.

This fiery off-shoot of the Campbell line took time to settle down as country lairds. The 11th Thane was murdered, the 12th went to war with the west-coast clans over ownership of Mull, and the 13th married a poisoner who is said to have killed off three guests at a single supper. The Thane himself was certified insane in 1639, perhaps as a result of wifely potions.

Above The drawing room was once the Great Hall at Cawdor Castle, built during the 16th century. It has seen many changes over the centuries, including the addition, in 1684, of a massive stone fireplace decorated with the Cawdor emblems of a stag's head and buckle.

Given such behaviour, and with the nation in a state of civil war, the castle's upkeep took a low priority. Nonetheless, a new range was added in the 1640s and there were more extensive changes later in the century, when the 15th Thane reworked the old fortress into a more elegant and comfortable form. The castle then slept again.

In the early 18th century, the family acquired vast estates in Wales, leaving Cawdor in the care of factors. So unlike many ancient castles, it was neither replaced with a modern mansion, nor 'improved'. There were some Baronial additions made by the 1st Earl in the 1850s and by the 2nd Earl a generation later, but they were restrained and respectful of the genuinely old. Their main effect is to give an external appearance of order and coherence that the castle's rambling interior belies.

Cluttered, quirky and designed for living rather than for show, the rooms have enormous charm. The 16th-century Great Hall is now a comfortable drawing room, while the Tower Room upstairs is more appealing still for its cosy informality. The Thanes have acquired some remarkable possessions in the course of their rumbustious lives – fine antiques, curiosities and weapons, pictures both old and modern. The set of tapestries illustrating the misadventures of Don Quixote seems particularly suited to the house – or at least to its quixotic owners.

Duart castle

★ ★ ★ The ancient Maclean stronghold, restored by an Edwardian descendant

On the Isle of Mull, 8 miles NW of Oban; private house, open part year

Perched on a rocky crag on the south-east tip of Mull, the ancestral seat of the Macleans stands guard over the sea-lanes of the west highland coast. The castle dates back to the 13th century, when possession of the Hebrides was still disputed between Scottish and Norse kings and local warlords pursued vendettas of their own. It was restored from a state of ruin in the early 1900s.

At some early date, beyond the reach of certain history, Duart belonged to the MacDougalls of Lorn, who built the curtain wall to enclose timber buildings that have long since disappeared. In the 14th century, MacDougall power waned and their castles passed to the MacDonald Lords of the Isles, who in turn gave Duart to the Macleans as part of a marriage settlement. It was, most probably, Lachlan Maclean who built the four-storey keep in around 1390, with further ranges being added up until the 1670s.

'... a stronghold from which
to wage bloody feuds...'

For some three hundred years, Duart provided the Maclean chiefs with a stronghold from which to wage their bloody feuds against the neighbouring MacDonalds and Campbells. It was not until the reign of James VI that, like other Hebridean chiefs, they were brought to heel and lost their virtual independence from the Scottish realm.

When Cromwell invaded Scotland, the Macleans backed King Charles; three English warships were wrecked beneath the castle battlements in the attempt to seize the clan's 10-year-old Chief. But in the long term such proud sea-fortresses were doomed – as was the Celtic tribal culture of the isles. Broken by debt and dispute with the all-powerful Earls of Argyll, the Macleans finally surrendered their estates in 1691, condemned as Jacobite conspirators. The castle then served as a military garrison, until it was abandoned in 1751.

But even as their castle crumbled, the chiefs of Clan Maclean were finding a new role. Throughout the 18th and the 19th centuries they pursued successful military careers. They married well, invested wisely and eventually grew rich. In 1911, Sir Fitzroy Maclean, the 26th Chief, bought back the castle and began the massive task of restoration. The architect John Burnet was not required to produce a precise re-creation of the past, as conservation agencies would now insist. His brief was to bring Duart back to life, both as a home and as a centre for the clan. Today, the castle still serves both these functions admirably and is, in addition, one of Mull's most popular attractions.

The rooms on view are all in the medieval tower. Aside from the 'dungeons', complete with dummy prisoners, there is no attempt to hide the truth – that this is an Edwardian home created within an ancient shell. Two contrasting rooms stand out. One is the Banqueting Hall, a great beamed chamber with windows cut through 9-foot thick walls that somehow manages to be both baronial and homely. The other is known as the Sea Room – a glassed veranda with stupendous views across the Sound of Mull.

Dun Carloway

A partly preserved Iron Age tower

15 miles NW of Stornoway, Isle of Lewis; Historic Scotland, open all year

Brochs such as Dun Carloway remain one of prehistoric Scotland's greatest enigmas. It stands close by the shore, like many of its type, on what was once a busy sea-lane. It was built, around 2000 years ago, by some long-forgotten people who were mysteriously skilled in constructing towers of stone that achieved colossal strength within a delicate curvaceous form. Most intriguing of all, Dun Carloway prefigures by more than a millennium – some 13 centuries – essential aspects of the Scottish tower house. It even has a staircase and chambers built into its wall. Nothing remotely similar to brochs were built anywhere else in Iron Age Europe, and even within Scotland such architecture flourished only briefly before the skills involved were lost.

Although the tower has been plundered for stone, a section of wall stands fairly well preserved, some 30-foot high and tapering elegantly from its massive base. A low-roofed guard cell, perhaps intended for a dog, opens off the entry passage. Further doorways in the central court lead to cells within the wall and stairs that wind to narrow passageways above. The court, most probably, was roofed and may have had timber galleries overlooking the hearth and feasting-space below. Like medieval towers, Dun Carloway was designed to withstand raids rather than a siege. Its colossal form must also have expressed its owner's power and prestige.

Dunrobin castle

★ ★ ★ ★   A ducal seat of palatial proportions

Near Golspie, 8 miles NE of Dornoch; private house, open part year

The vast, multi-pinnacled chateau of Dunrobin towers improbably above the Dornoch Firth in an extravagant celebration of Scottish history and English wealth. The Earls of Sutherland began the castle in the 13th century and the tower they built still stands, embedded deep within the palace. They married well, forging links with royalty, and hung onto their lands through wars, law-suits and rebellions. Despite their lineage and lands, it took until 1785 for them to break through into the first division of influence and wealth: that was the year that 19-year-old Countess Elizabeth married George Granville Leveson-Gower, the heir to the obscenely rich Marquess of Stafford.

George succeeded to his English title in 1803 and was made the 1st Duke of Sutherland in 1833. He died shortly afterwards and a gigantic statue, more than ten times life-size, was erected on a hill above Golspie to commemorate the improvements he made to Elizabeth's estate. But he is more commonly remembered for the brutal evictions that he sanctioned in the name of progress, forcibly 'resettling' more than 5000 tenants in the most infamous of all the highland clearances.

It was the 2nd Duke, together with his wife the Duchess Harriet, who transformed the castle into one of Scotland's grandest stately homes. Along with their other houses – including Trentham Hall in Staffordshire, Cliveden in Buckinghamshire and what is now Lancaster House in London – Dunrobin was reworked as a modern palace suitable for one of the richest and noblest families in Britain. With eight children and innumerable relatives, besides most of fashionable society claiming to be friends, they needed

'... it is still **a breathtaking sight.**'

Above Queen Victoria visited Dunrobin in 1872. Although the room she slept in no longer exists – it became part of the new library after the 1915 fire – the bed made especially for her still survives. It stands in the Green and Gold Room, redecorated in a French style in 1921 for the Duchess Eileen, wife of the 5th Duke.

ample space in which to entertain. Advised by their favourite architect, Charles Barry, they tripled the size of the existing castle and changed its face as drastically as if they were building from scratch. Dunrobin mingles the chateaux of the Loire and the dreams of Bavaria's mad King Ludwig, with a seasoning of Scots Baronial thrown in. It was even more spectacular before Lorimer trimmed down some of its excesses in the 1920s, but it is still a breathtaking sight. There are few other houses that so forcibly express the iron-willed self-confidence of Victorian Britain's land-owning plutocracy. Only a cynic would complain that it looks a touch like Disneyland.

The interior, although impressive, is sadly lacking the patina of age. Almost no medieval or Renaissance features survive and even the Victorian decor was largely destroyed by a fire in 1915. Luckily, the family's furniture and paintings escaped the blaze, since the castle had been stripped of

Above The main staircase at Dunrobin was designed to impress; a stately stairway leading up to the important reception rooms on the first floor. Stag's heads mounted on the walls among the family portraits are reminders of the days when the castle would have served as a base for aristocratic hunting trips.

its contents to serve as a wartime naval hospital. When peace returned, the damaged rooms were restored by Robert Lorimer, displaying his trademark passion for traditional craftsmanship and detail.

The entrance is magnificently arrogant. Visitors are confronted on arrival with a huge armorial panel displaying the family's assorted crests and arms: both Robert the Bruce and Henry VII feature on this stone-carved record of top-flight Anglo-Scottish ancestry. From the inner hall, an imposing stone staircase, lined with hunting trophies including an entire stuffed red stag, leads up to the *piano-nobile* reception rooms. Here, the Renaissance-style moulded ceilings are Lorimer's, as is the panelling in sycamore. The overall effect is of opulence, with portraits of the family on every wall.

The drawing room, created by Lorimer from two smaller rooms, is vast and coldly formal. It is furnished with ornate French pieces arranged for display rather than use. Elsewhere, there are rooms to answer every need and whim – a music room, breakfast room, library, ladies' sitting room (ideal for embroidery and gossip), a study, a seamstress's room, the list goes on and on. And these are just the rooms on public view.

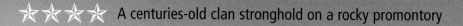

★★★★☆ A centuries-old clan stronghold on a rocky promontory

14 miles from Portree, Isle of Skye; private house, open all year

When Dr Johnson stayed at Dunvegan in 1773, during his tour of the Hebrides with Boswell, he was uncharacteristically enthusiastic in his praise. He had, he later wrote, 'tasted lotus' as a guest of the MacLeods and was most unwilling to depart. It was not just the hospitality that so delighted him. Nor was it the contrast that their 'partly old and partly modern' castle presented to the inns where he had previously lodged. It was rather that Dunvegan provided all that he had hoped to find when he set out on his tour – stirring history and ancient legends, romantic relics and a glimpse

Dunvegan castle

Above The walls of the dining room are hung with portraits of past clan chiefs, including one of the 28th chief, Dame Flora MacLeod. A passionate advocate of clan interests, Dame Flora established the Clan MacLeod Parliaments in 1956. Held every four years, delegates from MacLeod societies worldwide meet at Dunvegan to discuss clan matters.

into the fast-disappearing patriarchal culture of the clans. For today's visitors, the castle still holds much the same appeal. Dunvegan is the oldest continually inhabited castle in the Highlands and it continues to exert a glamorous allure.

The true age of the castle is as uncertain as the origins of the MacLeods. The site – a steep basalt rock surrounded by water on three sides – was probably a Norse stronghold, or dun, named after a warrior called Began. More certain history begins in the mid-13th century, when Skye formed part of the territories of Leod Olafson, a son of the last Norse king of Man. With a Viking for a father and a Scots heiress for a wife, plus no doubt some Pictish and a touch of Irish in his veins, Leod was a typical warlord of the west. Establishing Dunvegan as his seat of power, he built a high stone wall around the rock, with a ditch on the landward side and an entrance facing out to sea. His sons called themselves MacLeods and all who lived under their protection did likewise. Thus the castle and the clan were formed.

If truth be told, neither played a major role in Scotland's medieval history, for the MacLeods were always more concerned with local feuds than national affairs. Their greatest rivals were their neighbours, the Macdonalds of Clanranald, linked to the powerful Lordship of the Isles. As late as 1577, a MacLeod raiding party slaughtered the entire population of Eigg, some 400 people. The following year, the Macdonalds exacted their revenge, torching a church near Dunvegan while the MacLeods were celebrating Mass.

'... the oldest continually inhabited castle in the Highlands continues to exert a glamorous allure.'

In the light of this bloody history, it is not surprising that Dunvegan was so strongly fortified. The castle today is still defined by its ancient curtain wall and two medieval structures have survived – the massive keep dating from the 14th century and the tower house, known as the Fairy Tower, of *c*1500. By the time of Dr Johnson's visit the keep lay in ruins and new ranges had been built, with further improvements made towards the end of the 18th century. Finally, in the 1840s, came the inevitable Romantic reconstruction. The keep was rebuilt with a soaring tower, battlements were added and history was reclaimed. Unlike the majority of Highland chiefs, the MacLeods were able to hang onto their home, although financial challenges meant that it was rented out for more than 80 years. The redoubtable 28th clan chief, Dame Flora, brought the castle back to life in the 1930s.

On the outside, coarse harling resembling concrete conceals most of the original exterior details. The rooms on public view are, for the most part, reception rooms with Georgian or Victorian decor, although there are, of course, medieval cellars and a dungeon on show. The real interest lies in the objects on display. Ranging from prehistoric artefacts to Jacobite relics, they embody the mystique of both castle and clan. The Horn of Rory Mor is a drinking vessel, holding almost two bottles of wine, that new chiefs had to drain in a single draught. The most prized possession of the MacLeods is the legendary Fairy Flag, a fragment of silk of ethereal fragility, on display in the drawing room.

Below The famous Fairy Flag, mounted in a frame, hangs in the drawing room. Legend has it that the flag was left at the castle by the fairy wife of a clan chief as magical protection for her children when she was forced to return to her own kind. It came to be believed that the flag, when raised, could save members of the MacLeod clan from disaster.

Eilean Donan castle

★★★ The archetypal Highland castle, set on its own island

At Dornie, 8 miles E of Kyle of Lochalsh; private house, open part year

Set on a rocky islet at the junction of three sea lochs, Eilean Donan is outlandishly picturesque. It is also an unapologetic fiction – a visionary re-creation built up from ruins less than a century ago. Yet it looks utterly magnificent against its backdrop of soul-stirring scenery, and as such is accepted as a national treasure.

The site has seen strongholds come and go since prehistoric times. It was a base for Pictish and Norse warlords before becoming a walled castle during the medieval Lordship of the Isles. By the 14th century the castle was held by the Mackenzies of Kintail and later by the Macraes. In 1719 it was briefly garrisoned by Spanish troops supporting a Jacobite uprising: it was shelled by the Royal Navy, then blown up until reduced to little more than rubble.

That should have been the end of the story, but in 1912 the ruins were bought by Lt. Colonel Macrae-Gilstrap, who set about reconstructing it into a modern home. Although there was an architect involved – the little-known G. M. Watson – it was the clerk of works, Farquhar Macrae, who oversaw the building in every detail. It is said that the medieval lay-out was revealed to Macrae in dreams, a story unlikely to impress Historic Scotland – such tinkering with an historic monument would never be allowed today.

The exterior of the castle is a reasonably accurate reconstruction, aside from the little bridge that links the castle with the shore and a rather curious veranda. A tunnel-vaulted entrance hall sets the scene indoors, with narrow windows cut through 14-foot-thick stone and much weaponry on show. Up a narrow flight of stairs, the Great Hall is a splendidly impressive chamber with bare rubble walls, wooden beams and a vast Gothic fireplace. There are even spy-holes high up in the walls through which a chief could keep an eye on guests. Bedrooms on the floor above are more honestly Edwardian, genuine mementoes of a vanished age. The castle was a place in which the Macrae-Gilstraps and their guests could indulge in a fantasy of Jacobites and clans. It is a wonderful example of architecture's power to express a dream.

'... utterly magnificent against its backdrop of soul-stirring scenery.'

Above The Great Hall at Eilean Donan is not the medieval room it seems – it is a 20th-century creation. The massive timber beams supporting the roof are made from Douglas fir trees that grew in British Columbia; they were donated to the castle during its restoration by the Canadian branch of the Macrae clan. The modern carpet features a Macrae tartan.

Fort George

✯ ✯ ✯ An extensive Georgian fortress on the Moray Firth

11 miles NE of Inverness; Historic Scotland, open all year

Above The barracks at Fort George were built to form streets, ranged around a central parade ground. They offered accommodation to 1600 men in two infantry battalions. Today the fort is home to the Black Watch.

Massively fortified and colossal in scale, Fort George is an outstanding example of 18th-century military engineering and a monument to Highland history. It is still a working barracks, with soldiers often outnumbering tourists, yet the whole complex has survived in such immaculate originality that one half expects to see 'redcoats' marching by instead of squaddies in fatigues.

Built in the aftermath of the 1745 Jacobite uprising, the fort was intended as a garrison that would discourage further unrest in the Highlands. Covering 42 acres and with almost a mile of ramparts, it was designed to withstand a full-scale attack by a large, sophisticated army, incorporating all the latest thinking on artillery and siege warfare. The effectiveness of the defences can readily be seen – Fort George was meant not only to intimidate the Highlanders, but also to impress any French who might happen to sail past with invasion in mind. The complex took more than twenty years to build and the final cost of over £200,000 was greater than Scotland's entire annual economic output at the time.

Quite apart from the elaborate defences, the fort is fascinating for its architectural design. The contractors for the project were William Adam and his brilliant family, but the actual architect was Major General William Skinner, an otherwise unknown military engineer. He laid out the barrack blocks in the manner of a Roman legionary camp, with a grid of streets and a vista down the central axis terminating in an archway and a church. The buildings are symmetrical and classical, with pavilion blocks at each end. Subtleties of rank (officers had larger window-panes), are expressed within palatial, unified façades. It all amounted to an orderly, efficient and aesthetically attractive mini-city, not dissimilar to Edinburgh's New Town.

Aside from museums, a weaponry collection and mess halls converted into cafes, three historic barrack rooms are open to the public. The earliest replicates conditions in 1780, when rank-and-file soldiers slept eight to a room and two to a bed, cooking their own meals on the fire. There is an officer's room of 1813, spacious but distinctly spartan, and finally another rank-and-file room of 1868, to show how conditions had improved.

Having been designed to repel Highland clans, Fort George soon became a centre for recruiting Highland regiments. Within a generation of Culloden there were kilted clansmen in the fort, training as soldiers that would defend the British Empire. No shot has ever been fired in anger from its walls.

'Fort George was meant ... to **intimidate** the Highlanders ...'

Hugh Miller's cottage

★ The modest birthplace of a pioneering geologist

At Cromarty, 16 miles NE of Inverness; National Trust for Scotland, open part year

Creative, moralistic, opinionated, tormented by religious doubt – Hugh Miller was a genius of a particularly Scottish kind. At the time of his suicide in 1856, he was famous as a pioneering geologist seeking the origins of life, but he is now pretty much forgotten. The National Trust for Scotland has made every effort to put right this oversight in their restoration of his birthplace.

The cottage itself is a little gem. Built of whitewashed cob and roofed in thatch, it would not look out of place in Devon – nor, indeed, would the village street on which it stands. Dating from the early 18th century, the house is now presented as it may have looked at the time of Miller's birth in 1802. Some of the original furniture remains, including the 'girnel' for storing oatmeal, with a drawer for the slices of cold porridge that sustained Miller on his adolescent rambles. In keeping with the man himself, there is an emphasis on 'education' and a great many fossils on display.

Although modest in scale and rather prim, this is a place worth seeing for its simple charm. Historically, it is also a rare survival of its type, its preservation being due entirely to its long-established, if little-known, status as a shrine. A grander house next door, Miller's home in later life, serves as a more conventional museum.

Inveraray castle

★★★★☆ A Georgian castle with an unusual blending of styles

At Inveraray, 19 miles SE of Oban; private house, open part year

Inveraray is the most untypical of Scottish castles. At the time of its construction, in the mid-18th century, it resembled no other house in Britain and has remained pretty much unique ever since. Mingling Classical and Gothick themes, it looks like an English mansion crossed with a French chateau to produce a magnificent over-sized toy fort. Puzzling and palatial, in a wild, remote location, it is a house with many teasing riddles to explain. As usual in the Highlands, history holds the key.

For centuries, the Campbells led one of two opposing groups that fought for control of the western highlands. From the time of Robert the Bruce, they sided with Scotland's kings against their neighbours, the Macdonalds, and the old Norse-Gaelic culture of the Lordship of the Isles. Originally based at Innis Chonnel on Loch Awe, they moved their power base to Inveraray in the mid-15th century, at around the time that the Campbell chiefs first became Earls of Argyll. Later Earls were prominent Scottish courtiers, accumulating vast estates and steadily increasing their power both as statesmen in Edinburgh and as warlords in Argyll. Even the execution for High Treason of two successive Earls, in 1661 and 1685, failed to dent the family's prestige. Nor did the Glencoe Massacre

INVERARAY

Above The Armoury Hall rises up through the heart of the castle, its walls bristling with antique weapons. **Right** The State Dining Room was decorated in the 1780s with wall paintings by two French artists, Girard and Guinand. **Far right** The set of 18th-century Beauvais tapestries in the Tapestry Drawing Room were specifically made for the room.

of 1692, when a Campbell regiment was sent to exact governmental vengeance on the Jacobite Macdonalds of Glencoe in what many still regard, perhaps unfairly, as the last act in an ancient feud.

In the early years of the 18th century, the 10th Earl of Argyll, who had supported William and Mary's claim to the Crown, was made 1st Duke. His eldest son, the 2nd Duke, was a Field Marshal in the British army who became known as *Ian Ruadh nan cath* – Red John of the Battles – to his Gaelic-speaking troops; he helped to negotiate the Union with England. When John died in 1743 the title passed to his brother, the Earl of Ilay. The 3rd Duke was 61 years old, had recently retired from a public life dominating Scottish politics, and was looking for some fresh challenge to occupy his time. As soon as he succeeded to the dukedom, he threw himself wholeheartedly into a project to 'improve' the clan seat at Inveraray.

It was a massively ambitious undertaking. Inveraray at the time was a squalid little town, noted largely for its sixty drinking dens. Under the Duke's scheme, a new town was to be built half a mile along the shore. Roads and bridges would link this modern Inveraray with the outside world and the whole way of life would be radically transformed by industry, trade and agricultural improvements. But the first and, symbolically, most important aspect of the scheme was the building of a suitably impressive ducal seat to replace the tumble-down old tower house that was Inveraray Castle.

INVERARAY

The architect was Roger Morris, generally better known for his Palladian designs. William Adam and his sons were overseers and the foundation stone was laid in October 1746. The inspiration for the unusual design remains obscure. Vanbrugh is sometimes held responsible, having some years earlier sketched a little 'toy-fort' banqueting pavilion for the military 2nd Duke. But it was almost certainly the 3rd Duke, rather than an architect, who in defiance of convention decided that this ornamental style was suited to a full-sized house. The house remained unfinished when the 3rd Duke died in 1761 and it was not until the 1780s that the 5th Duke was finally able to move in. There were some alterations following a fire in the 1870s – the turrets acquired their pointy roofs at this time and an attic storey was added to the roof. But despite a further fire in 1975, Inveraray has remained remarkably unchanged as an 18th-century stately home.

The decor in the state rooms is amongst the finest of its kind, with delicately painted designs creating a sophisticated, feminine and distinctly French ambience. The Armoury Hall, on the other hand, is a chest-thumping fantasy of male power, with 1500 guns, pikes and halberds displayed on the walls of a soaring top-lit atrium, flanked by matching staircase halls to either side. Here, the intention behind the castle's design is made clear. Inveraray was to be a clan seat for the Age of Reason. The tower that rises from the roofline is a fortress at the heart of a refined chateau – a reminder that the Duke could, if needs must, raise 5000 clansmen to his cause as readily as he could throw a supper party. Today, the castle still remains a focus for the globally enormous Campbell clan.

Inveraray jail INVERARAY

INVERARAY

☆ Re-creation of a 19th-century prison

At Inveraray, 19 miles SE of Oban; museum, open all year

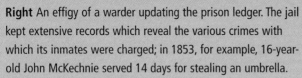

Right An effigy of a warder updating the prison ledger. The jail kept extensive records which reveal the various crimes with which its inmates were charged; in 1853, for example, 16-year-old John McKechnie served 14 days for stealing an umbrella.

When the 3rd Duke of Argyll began to redevelop Inverary in the mid-18th century, John Adam provided the new town with an elegant 'Town House' that was to serve both as a courthouse and a prison. By the early 1800s this attractive but quite modest building was considered inadequate and out of date. There were particular objections to the grilled arcade in which prisoners were held on full display to passers-by.

A new courthouse, with a purpose-built prison block hidden in the yard behind, was designed in 1820 by James Gillespie Graham. Further cells were added in 1848, when the overcrowded jail was reformed in response to marginally more humanitarian ideas about how such institutions should be run. The prison closed in 1889 and the whole complex was eventually abandoned, until it was rescued and restored by the Scottish Office in the 1980s.

The jail is now a tourist attraction, complete with the usual sound effects, mannequins and guides dressed as warders. It is all rather sanitized, but highly educational and rather fun. In the courtroom a trial is in session, and visitors sit next to costumed dummies. In the prison blocks cells have been refurbished to show how conditions changed over the years, from hugger-mugger squalor to the spotless misery of solitary confinement. Mannequins are posed picking oakum and knitting herring nets. Visitors can turn the crank that provided the most useless form of labour – if a warder was mean-minded, he could 'turn the screw' to make it harder. There is even a whipping table and birch-rod, with a sign that says 'please try'. You'd never get such service from the National Trust.

Jarlshof

★★ An island settlement displaying thousands of years of history

22 miles S of Lerwick, Shetland; Historic Scotland, open part year

The ruins of Jarlshof span some 4000 years, from the 3rd millennium BC to the 17th century. Although it is unlikely that occupation was continuous, the settlement presents a palimpsest of Shetland history. The site is impressive but somewhat confusing, with structures from different periods overlying and interlacing each other. The oldest, Neolithic houses are mere fragments built into middens of domestic rubbish, seen much better at Skara Brae (see page 152). Nearby, a slightly later and more substantial house was rebuilt as a bronze-smith's workshop in about 800BC.

Moving on a few more centuries (and walking a few yards), three stone roundhouses remain from an Iron Age farm. Two of them have 'souterrains' – underground passages – the purpose of which has never been satisfactorily explained. The farmstead must have prospered for the inhabitants built a broch, the ultimate expression of Iron Age power and prestige. Sadly, half of the broch has disappeared over the cliff. Some prehistoric restoration work has confused this part of the site, but this is, nonetheless, the most intriguing corner of Jarlshof, with high-walled, secluded spaces that can still be imagined as homes.

The Norse settlement, by contrast, looks misleadingly straightforward: it is actually even harder to unravel. The maze of grass-capped foundations represents an overlapping series of longhouses, cattle byres and other buildings, including a small sauna, that span hundreds of years of occupation, from AD850 to about 1275. Lastly, skipping the remains of a medieval hall, there is the house built in 1604 by Patrick, Earl of Orkney. This is 'the Old House at Sumburgh', portrayed as the 'Jarlshof' (Earl's House) in Sir Walter Scott's novel, *The Pirate*. Its roofless shell dominates the site, the last chapter of the settlement's story.

'The ruins of **Jarlshof** span some **4000 years** ...
a palimpsest of **Shetland history.**'

Kinloch castle

★ ★ ★ A castle-style mansion preserved in an Edwardian time-warp

On Rum, 17 miles W of Mallaig; private house, open for tours by arrangement

Kinloch Castle is a fading dream of Edwardian elegance. The battlemented red sandstone mansion was built in 1897 for George Bullough, who had inherited the Isle of Rum, together with a cotton fortune, from his father. The house cost £250,000 to build – more than £14 million in modern terms – and further extravagant improvements were made in 1903 when George married a feisty divorcee, reputedly a mistress of King Edward VII. Their fake castle was equipped with every modern gadget that money could buy: electric lighting, telephones, even an early form of air conditioning.

'To enter the castle is to step back in time.'

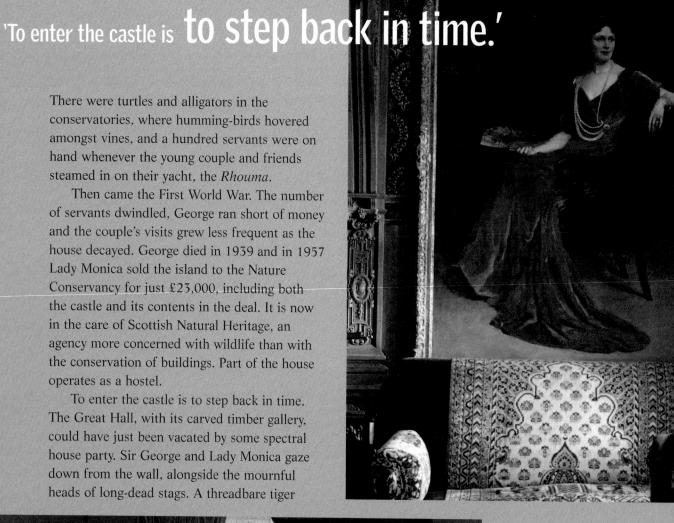

There were turtles and alligators in the conservatories, where humming-birds hovered amongst vines, and a hundred servants were on hand whenever the young couple and friends steamed in on their yacht, the *Rhouma*.

Then came the First World War. The number of servants dwindled, George ran short of money and the couple's visits grew less frequent as the house decayed. George died in 1939 and in 1957 Lady Monica sold the island to the Nature Conservancy for just £23,000, including both the castle and its contents in the deal. It is now in the care of Scottish Natural Heritage, an agency more concerned with wildlife than with the conservation of buildings. Part of the house operates as a hostel.

To enter the castle is to step back in time. The Great Hall, with its carved timber gallery, could have just been vacated by some spectral house party. Sir George and Lady Monica gaze down from the wall, alongside the mournful heads of long-dead stags. A threadbare tiger

Above A portrait of Lady Monica looks down over the Great Hall.
Right After George Bullough's marriage to Monica in 1903, the Great Hall was grandly furnished with pieces ordered from the fashionable firms of Warings and Shoolbred.
Left Kinloch Castle was built with every possible modern convenience of the day. The bathrooms were fitted with the most sophisticated plumbing available and the rooms were lit by electricity, generated by a dam at nearby Coire Dubh.

skin sprawls across the floor between a moth-eaten sofa and a life-size bronze eagle that was a present from the Emperor of Japan. The lid of the Steinway grand piano bears the scars of dancing heels. Beneath the stairs stands an orchestrion, an electric version of a fairground organ, that blasts out marches and waltzes with relentless jollity. The dining room, drawing room and billiard room are all equally extraordinary, filled with mementoes of a vanished world. The ballroom has high windows and a double-sided serving hatch to ensure the total privacy of dancers, with the orchestra playing from behind closed curtains. Almost nothing has been altered since the early 1900s. Even the plumbing in the bathrooms, with water-jets and douches, is original.

In 2003 the castle just failed to win the BBC's Restoration contest. Since then, Prince Charles has expressed his support and his building renovation charity, the Prince's Regeneration Trust, is exploring options for the future. Despite estimated costs of £8 million there is optimism that the project will proceed. Otherwise, Kinloch Castle may be lost for ever.

Kisimul castle

⭐ A much-restored medieval harbour castle

At Castlebay, just off the Isle of Barra; Historic Scotland, open part year

From a distance, Kisimul Castle looks superb. It rises from a rock in the harbour of Castlebay, the Isle of Barra's village 'capital', giving the appearance of a perfectly preserved medieval fortress. It may date back to the 12th or even the 11th century, although an architectural historian might disagree.

Myths and legends swirl around the battlemented walls, for this is the ancient seat of the Macneils, who claim descent from Irish kings. For centuries, their galleys were feared throughout the Hebrides and their stronghold of Kisimul was equally renowned. And although the Macneils suffered the same fate of other clans, with their lands being sold and their castle falling into ruin, Kisimul was eventually saved.

In 1937 Robert Macneil, a wealthy American with architectural ambitions, was accepted as the 45th clan chief. He payed a flying visit to Barra then bought the ruined castle. Ten years later he began an ambitious restoration project that continued until his death in 1970. Using found materials and local labour, the breaches in the curtain wall were patched, floors were inserted in the tower and long-vanished buildings rose once more. Thanks to the efforts of Robert Macneil, the castle is now one of the premier attractions in the Western Isles.

Yet Macneil had shortcomings, both as an architect and conservator. He brought the ruin back to life, but the castle is neither a truly convincing re-creation nor an appealing modern home. The tower remains virtually a shell, with bare platform floors. The Tanist's House, built from scratch as Macneil's own suite, is little more than a pokey cottage. Across the courtyard in the hall, a few rusty muskets hang from dripping walls. Up close, it is a touch depressing.

In 2000 Macneil's son, the 46th chief (if the genealogy is to be believed), handed Kisimul over to Historic Scotland on a thousand-year lease at an annual rent of £1 and a bottle of whisky. There are no plans to make further alterations. For all its oddities, Macneil's work is now considered an intrinsic part of Kisimul's history and character.

Mount Stuart

★ ★ ★ ★ A spectacular Victorian-Gothic fantasy palace

5 miles S of Rothesay, Isle of Bute; private house, open part year

John Patrick Crichton-Stuart, 3rd Marquess of Bute, was a man of passionate enthusiasms matched by enormous wealth. Orphaned as an infant, he came of age in 1868, inheriting huge estates in Scotland and Wales with an annual income of some £300,000. He used his money well. As a lover of all things old, beautiful and strange, he became a one-man conservation agency, restoring ruinous medieval buildings to a state of Gothic splendour that matched his own vision of Arthurian romance.

In Wales, he rebuilt Castell Coch and Cardiff Castle. In Scotland, Falkland Palace (see page 27) was the most significant of many historic structures that he helped to save. But perhaps the most spectacular of all his projects was the reconstruction of Mount Stuart, his family seat on the Isle of Bute. The old house – a somewhat dour-looking mansion dating from the early 18th century – burnt down in 1877. Within months, Bute had commissioned a replacement from Robert Rowand Anderson, an architect who shared his medievalist passions. No expense was spared on materials, the finest craftsmen were employed and every modern luxury was provided. The Marquess kept no record of the costs involved, but it was certainly one of the most extravagant houses of the age and details still remained to be finished at the time of his death in 1900.

Above The painting on the ceiling of the Horoscope Room records the position of the stars and planets on 12 September, 1847, the day the 3rd Marquess was born. The bed, an addition made in the 1980s, is carved with representations of Night and Day. **Right** In the drawing room, the ceiling is painted with the coats of arms of the male descendants of the 2nd Marquess. On the walls are paintings by old masters such as Titian, Tintoretto and Veronese.

Built of rich pink sandstone, with arched windows and a tall pitched roof, the house is an eclectic mix of Gothic styles, faintly but unfortunately reminiscent of Victorian town halls. The exterior does nothing to prepare one for the sumptuous extravagance inside. The Marble Hall is breathtaking, rising to a height of 80 feet to form an internal cloister at the building's heart. The stonework is all rare Italian marble and alabaster. Each column capital is individually carved with leaves and flowers; a few, unfinished at the time the 3rd Marquess died, remain blank. From high above, light filters in through stained-glass windows, creating a mysterious cathedral gloom. All the main rooms of the house are accessed from this astonishing central space, with reception rooms on the *piano nobile* and bedrooms ranged around the galleries above. The drawing room is particularly spectacular with Gothic arches, a vast marble overmantel and a hand-carved heraldic ceiling set against a ground of polished mica. Quite clearly, the Marquess was not a subscriber to the idea that 'less is more'.

The house has continued to evolve, sometimes rather unpredictably. The 4th Marquess, though passionate about historic buildings, shared his generation's loathing for Victorian style. In 1920 he advertised Mount Stuart for sale as a kit of parts, to be demolished and rebuilt elsewhere 'as an Hotel, Hydro, Restaurant, Casino, Public Building, Etc'. Fortunately, he failed to find a buyer. Instead, he introduced some fine new contents, including the resplendent tapestries in the Marble Hall, which were hand-woven in the Dovecote Studios that he established in Edinburgh.

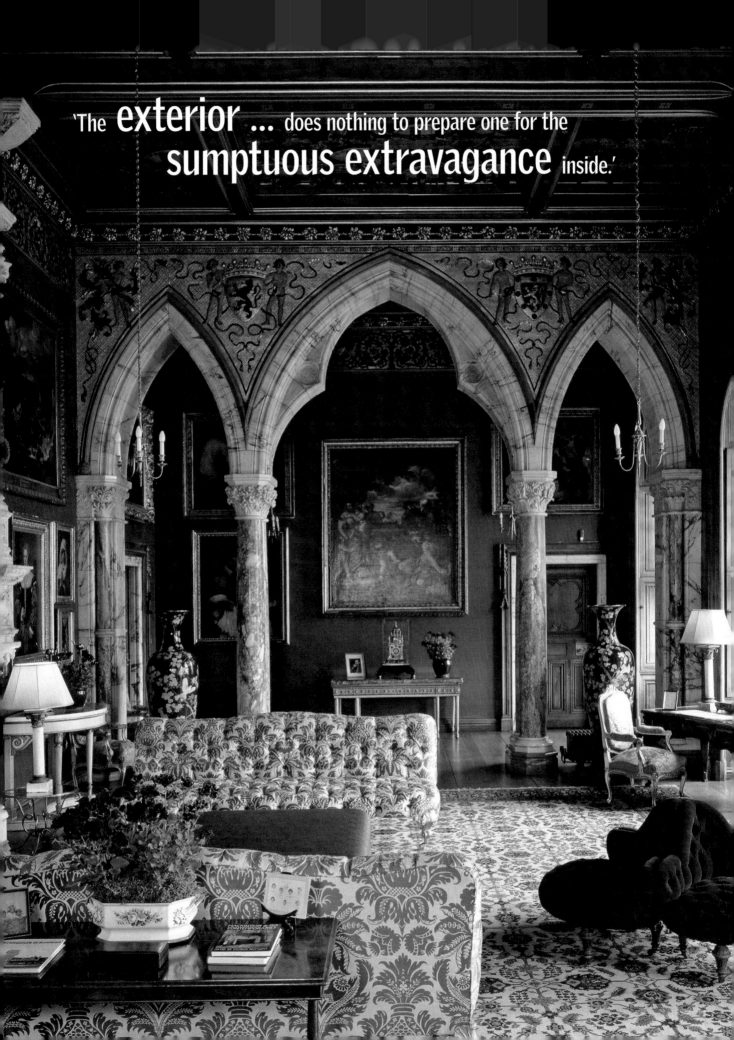

'The **exterior** ... does nothing to prepare one for the **sumptuous extravagance** inside.'

Above Mount Stuart was thoroughly up to date in its amenities. The swimming pool, fully tiled and spanned by a vaulted ceiling inspired by medieval architecture, was the first heated indoor pool in a private house in Britain. Electricity was laid on in 1883 – Mount Stuart was one of the first houses to have it – and telephones were installed in 1887.

His grandson, the 6th Marquess, was an ardent conservationist who served as chairman of the National Trust for Scotland. In the 1980s he and his wife gave the house a much-needed facelift, inside and out. Their mark is most apparent in the Horoscope Room, which had been the private sitting room of the 3rd Marquess, whose horoscope is painted on the ceiling. This became their bedroom, with the bed and other furnishings (in suitable medieval style) commissioned from contemporary craft workers. They also restored the room's *en suite* conservatory, which had lain derelict since being used as an operating theatre when the house was pressed into service as a naval hospital during the First World War. The current Marquess, a former racing driver who styles himself plain John Bute, remains committed to preserving the 'outrageous beauty' of his ancestral home.

This wildly eccentric house has now been owned, if not always loved, by five generations, but it remains a monument to the 3rd Marquess. It is that rare thing: a building that expresses its creator's obsessive and uncompromising will. There are many who will find it ugly or absurd, perhaps even a touch obscene. The 3rd Marquess would not give a fig for such views. Catholic and mystic, astrologist and scholar, aesthete, medievalist and champion of new technology, he was a multi-faceted man who threw himself heart and soul into the creation of his extraordinary home.

Broch of Gurness

The remains of an Iron Age stone tower and settlement

14 miles NW of Kirkwall, Orkney; Historic Scotland, open part year

Although not the tallest or best-preserved of brochs, the ruins at Gurness add up to one of Scotland's most fascinating Iron Age sites. The tower itself – constructed around 2000 years ago in the usual circular, hollow-walled form – is at the heart of a fortified, densely crowded settlement of stone-built houses, most of which survive to waist-height. The complex was surrounded by a rampart and multiple ditches, with impressive outerworks and a gated 'street' leading to the tower. At some point the broch partially collapsed and its remains were remodelled, adding extra layers of complexity.

Rather than attempt to disentangle the archaeological conundrum, it is better simply to drink in the Cyclopean splendours of the place. Despite the crude materials this is real architecture, carefully designed and intended to impress. In many ways it is similar to a medieval castle, although built a thousand years before. A further enigma is the stone-lined shaft, with steep steps and side-galleries, that bores deep under the broch's courtyard. Although leading to water, it appears too complicated to be just a well. Like most other brochs, Gurness was abandoned in the 2nd century AD. A later Pictish house, uncovered and demolished during excavations, has been reconstructed in a new position.

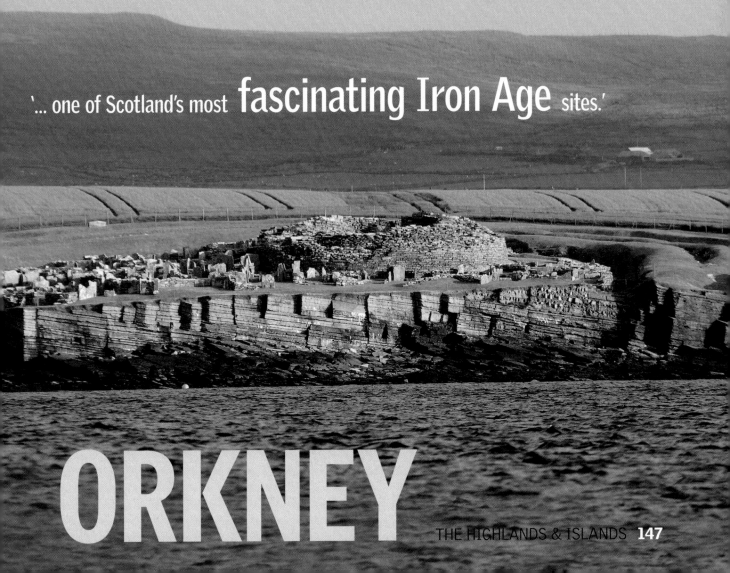

'... one of Scotland's most fascinating Iron Age sites.'

ORKNEY

Corrigall farm

An early 19th-century Orcadian farmstead, faithfully preserved

12 miles NW of Kirkwall, Orkney; museum, open part year

ORKNEY

There is a *Mary Celeste* quality to Corrigall Farm. This is no ordinary museum, but an eerily convincing evocation of an old Orcadian farmstead, built around 200 years ago and scarcely altered since. Externally, the family living accommodation looks little different from the animal byres and barns: a long, low cottage roofed with flagstones and turf. It is a classic 'but and ben', with one room for living in and another used for sleeping.

The living room looks well-used, with battered furniture and clutter on the shelves. A peat fire burns in the hearth and the aromatic smoke hangs heavy in the air. Chickens come and go, goats bleat in the yard and a cat is likely to be curled up on a wicker Orkney chair. The smaller, unheated room beyond contains box-beds, with storage space under the stone eaves. Clothing hangs from hooks and faded magazines lie scattered on a table. Most of the furniture is original to the house, while other contents have been gathered from elsewhere. Although every detail has been artfully arranged, it looks and feels as though nothing has moved since the place was a lively, overcrowded home.

Kirbuster farm

⭐ A rare historic farmhouse of a traditional type

20 miles NW of Kirkwall, Orkney; museum, open part year

The 'firehouse' at Kirbuster Farm is a unique survival of a type of home that was once commonplace throughout the Northern Isles. The house consists of one room, with a hearth in the centre of the floor. Beds are in recesses set within the thickness of the walls. The arrangement is scarcely different from the nearby prehistoric settlement at Skara Brae (see page 152), yet Kirbuster was lived in until 1961. By then, admittedly, the house had grown.

Additional accommodation was converted from outhouses sometime in the 19th century, when three generations were living cheek by jowl. These rooms, a parlour and bedroom, still remain decorated in Victorian style. According to parish records, one farmer at the time was publicly admonished for 'fornicating with a maid-servant in an upstairs room'. There is no upper floor, so presumably they were discovered in a hay-loft. In the yards outside, the corn-drying kiln and byres are now roofless shells. But with roots planted in the land as deep as those of any castle, Kirbuster exudes a certain primitive grandeur.

'... a unique survival ... one room with a **hearth** in the **centre** ...'

Kirkwall: **The Earl's** palace

★ The atmospheric ruins of a local despot's palace

Watergate, Kirkwall, Orkney; Historic Scotland, open part year

Patrick, Earl of Orkney, was a monster. Tyrannical, violent and treacherous, he ruled the Northern Isles like a despotic king, ignoring laws of God and man, just as his father had before him. In 1615 he was executed in Edinburgh for treason, along with his son. Four centuries later, we can at least admire the buildings he left behind.

As a patron of architecture, Patrick was a man of rare refinement, inspired by ideas well ahead of his time. His palaces and castles are now ruins – Scalloway in Shetland, Birsay and Kirkwall in Orkney. All are of interest, but Kirkwall is the best. Impressive as it is, the Earl's Palace was intended to be much larger, incorporating the old Bishop's Palace to one side within a twin-courtyard quadrangular design. From the vaulted ground floor, a broad staircase leads up to a series of intriguing rooms. One was for a steward, with a double-decker filing cupboard built into one wall. An ante-room displays a delicately decorated vault. The Great Hall is still magnificent despite its roofless state, lit by myriad windows of intricate, individual design. Beyond the withdrawing chamber, the Earl's bedchamber thrusts out to one side as a triple-aspect wing, with turreted closets in the corners. These private spaces could equally have served as lavatories or studies.

The use of light and space in the palace is quite breathtaking, given the early date of construction. Of course, such a project was only affordable because the Earl used slave labour, but great architects are seldom troubled by the human cost of their dreams. What mattered to the Earl was to leave proof of his genius and power in stone.

ORKNEY

Skaill house

★ The Laird of Skaill's mansion, built in the early 17th century

19 miles NW of Kirkwall, Orkney; private house, open part year

There has been a close link between Skaill House and its prehistoric neighbour, Skara Brae, ever since the 7th Laird of Skaill found the settlement exposed at the bottom of his garden following a ferocious storm in 1850. For many years, finds from the settlement were kept in the laird's dining room, while the stone-age homes were used as Wendy Houses by his children.

Skaill House itself dates from the 1620s when it was built for George Graham, Bishop of Orkney. Since then it has been altered and extended many times to form a rambling but pleasingly cohesive complex of mansion, outbuildings and yards. Although the family no longer use it as their home, care has been taken to maintain its personal, lived-in feel. The furniture is slightly worse-for-wear, books lie open on arm-chairs as though the reader has just popped into the kitchen to make a cup of tea.

The finds from Skara Brae have long ago been sent off to an Edinburgh museum, but there is still a family collection of militaria and curios tracing the house and its occupants back through the past 400 years. Skaill has no great architectural pretensions. It is an attractive, comfortable laird's house that offers an intriguing slice of social history.

Above The settlement at Skara Brae is made up of a group of eight dwellings, linked by low, roofed alleyways. When they were uncovered, ancient stone furniture still stood in place around a central hearth. In the 1920s, excavation work placed the settlement in the Iron Age, but in the 1970s this was revised to the much earlier Neolithic period.

★★★☆ Britain's oldest and best-preserved prehistoric village

19 miles NW of Kirkwall, Orkney; Historic Scotland, open all year

The settlement of Skara Brae was protected for millennia from the depredations of nature and man by a thick coating of wind-blown sand. Since its discovery, a great deal of money has been spent on excavating and presenting the prehistoric site, but now with 70,000 visitors a year it is sadly no longer possible to allow people to walk into the houses and touch furniture that has lasted for 5000 years. Instead, there is a designated path, with well-chosen viewpoints. This is one of Historic Scotland's finer efforts, with clear signage, helpful custodians and an interesting small museum. There is also a detailed reconstruction of one of the houses to give a 'hands-on' experience that helps one to make sense of the site and to appreciate its huge significance.

Unlike the great ritual monuments, such as Maes Howe or Stonehenge, Skara Brae tells of ordinary people and their everyday lives. The dwellings were not free-standing structures, they were built into a midden of old domestic waste – mollusc shells, bones, burnt cereals, rotted compost – and linked by tunnel-like stone corridors. The midden had accumulated over many years and would have provided good insulation from the wind and cold. The village was established *c*3100BC and then reconstructed about 300 years later, with slightly larger dwellings set still deeper into the mound, leaving only the roofs visible above ground. It was abandoned *c*2450BC and drifting sands then disguised its existence until a violent storm in 1850 revealed the tops of its ancient walls. The discovery came just in time. For thousands of years the sea has advanced into the bay to nibble at the site, which may once have been larger than it is today. What remains is now protected by a sea-wall.

The viewing path meanders through the village, often climbing the grass-cloaked bank of the midden to give close views of the rooms below. One house is separate from the mound and may have been some kind of meeting-house or workshop – or, as one custodian observed, perhaps the village pub. The other dwellings are virtually identical, each consisting of a single, spacious room with a

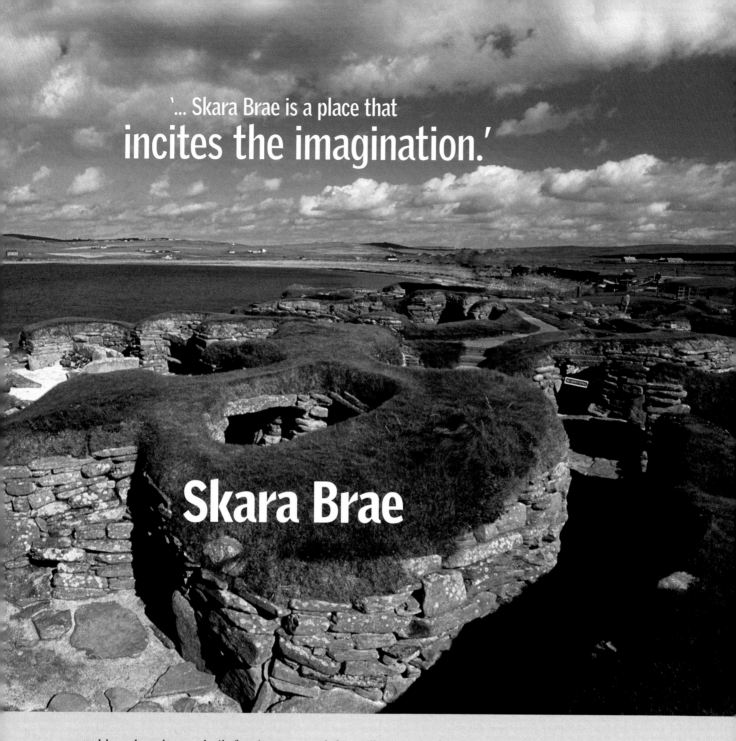

'... Skara Brae is a place that **incites the imagination.**'

Skara Brae

central hearth and stone-built furniture around the walls. It is the furniture that makes Skara Brae extraordinary. Box-beds and double-decked 'dressers' are constructed from smooth flagstones and every piece has a hand-finished look. Tanks set into the floor were originally lined with clay to make them water-tight, perhaps for storing live shell-fish or for warming water with hot stones. Bench-like slabs surround each hearth, with a throne-like seat – most likely for the head of the house – at the 'high' end opposite the door. Each home has a closet, almost certainly a privy, set into the thickness of the wall, with a well-constructed drain beneath its floor.

Standing in the replica of House 7, roofed with driftwood beams and turf, or walking on 5000-year-old stepping stones, one feels very close to the ancient villagers of Skara Brae. Many Orcadians lived in houses quite similar to these until recent times (see Kirbuster Farm, page 149), but there is much that we will never know about the people who once lived here. The distant past is a strange land that can never fully be understood, but Skara Brae is a place that incites the imagination.

Torosay castle

⭐ Victorian family home in Scots Baronial style

On the Isle of Mull, 9 miles W of Oban;
private house, open part year

Torosay Castle, a sturdy Baronial affair, was completed in 1858 for a Glaswegian sugar baron, Colonel Campbell of Possil. The architect was David Bryce, the foremost designer of country houses at the time, and no expense was spared in creating a comfortable modern mansion, situated at the heart of a large sporting estate. Yet Campbell sold up after just seven years and Torosay was purchased by the great-great-great uncle of the present owner.

Recent generations of the James family have had to fight to keep their home. Much of the estate has been sold off, and for a time they even ran the house as a hotel. Then in 1972 they took the brave decision to restore Torosay and open it to visitors. The appeal of the house lies in its originality. Little has changed in more than a century and the Victorian ambience has been preserved. Yet it is also a much loved and lived-in home. Sporting trophies, pictures, photographs and scrapbooks, plus all other possessions acquired over the generations, have much to say about the strong-willed, occasionally eccentric family that has tackled death duties and dry rot with equal determination.

And then there are the stunning gardens. Originally laid out in 1900, their beauty helps to explain why the family has found Torosay so impossible to leave.

☆ The ruins of an early medieval castle overlooking Loch Ness

Near Drumnadrochit, 14 miles SW of Inverness; Historic Scotland, open all year

Urquhart castle

Urquhart Castle is a hugely popular visitor attraction, although this may owe more to the legendary monster of Loch Ness than to the castle's architecture or historical associations. Spectacularly perched on a rocky promontory high above the loch – possibly on the site of a Pictish fort – the castle was begun in the 13th century by royal vassal, Sir Thomas Durward. It was to be a stronghold to defend his lands, situated as they were in dangerous disputed territory.

Centuries of conflict followed, with Urquhart Castle changing hands many times until it passed into the ownership of the Grants in recognition of their loyal service to the crown. They managed to enjoy a time of relative peace in the late 15th and early 16th centuries and the castle was rebuilt as a noble residence. But then, in 1692, a departing garrison of government troops set off a huge explosion that blew the gatehouse into fragments. Thereafter, what was left of the castle crumbled into picturesque ruin.

The remains are not easy to interpret, for they belong to different phases of the castle's long and rather messy history. Colossal chunks of masonry still lie around the wrecked gatehouse, and within the curtain wall a scene of devastation still greets the eye. The principal surviving structure is the 16th-century tower house, built by the Grants, and even this was partially destroyed by a storm in 1715. Of fairly modest scale, it stands within a well-protected inner close, with the cellar-height remains of other buildings in an outer yard. Elsewhere in the sprawling complex there are turrets, footings and enclosures that trace the castle back to its 13th-century beginnings. For all the beauty of its setting, Urquhart is intimidating, built to inspire respect with an image of brute strength.

Craigievar Castle

Northeast

The Northeast

Aberdeen:
Provost Skene's house

★★ An imposing town house built in the 16th century

Guestrow, Aberdeen; museum, open all year

A remarkable relic of old Aberdeen sits today among stark 1960s office-blocks. The building was originally the home of wealthy merchants who prospered from the city's European trade. In 1746 the Duke of Cumberland made it his temporary headquarters as he marched north. Later, the house hit hard times, becoming a common boarding-house. Its demolition was threatened during slum clearances in the 1930s, but happily this vandalism was thwarted by a popular campaign and, after lengthy restoration, Provost Skene's House opened to the public in 1953. More lavish refurbishment followed in the 1990s and the main rooms are now presented as a series of vignettes re-creating different periods of the building's history.

Although the house dates from the 16th century it takes its name from Sir George Skene, Provost of Aberdeen from 1676 to 1685. The Great Hall, parlour and bedroom have been furnished to reflect his occupation, and feature original details such as carved Renaissance fire-surrounds and delicately moulded plaster ceilings. Moving on, a richly panelled dining room and bedroom illustrate the opulence of the 18th-century mercantile class, and there is a small Regency parlour.

Some intriguing painted decor was discovered during restoration. In the Small Painted Gallery are miniature murals of classical landscapes, probably mid-18th century. On the top floor, a timber-ceilinged gallery is decorated with tempera-painted panels, celebrating a cult relating to the Wounds of Christ. They are thought to date from the 1620s, when the room must have been a Catholic chapel.

Ballindalloch castle

★★ An historic castle that has kept up with the times

14 miles NE of Grantown-on-Spey; private house, open part year

Despite its age, Ballindalloch is designed for modern living. Set in beautiful gardens beside the River Spey, it has been home to the same family since 1546 and has grown over the generations into a large, pleasant country house. Its core is a 16th-century Z-plan tower house, with slightly later upper floors in the elaborate, romantic style of Craigievar (see page 168). Two wings were added in the 1770s, another in the 1850s and nine more bedrooms in the 1870s, although these were demolished during a last transformation in the 1970s.

The Macpherson-Grants are still very much in residence and put every part of their enormous mansion to good use. There is some splendid furniture on show. The dining room, once the Great Hall of the tower house, is a Victorian extravaganza with richly carved panelling and a ceiling copied from Craigievar. The house also boasts one the finest collections of 17th-century Spanish paintings held in private hands, including works by Murillo and Velasquez. But unlike most historic houses open to the public, Ballindalloch is not hidebound to the past. Fitted carpets, comfy chairs and chintzy curtains sit happily alongside ancient heirlooms and heraldic carvings. There is a sense that house guests might arrive at any moment. Even the private bedrooms are on view. Instead of a vanished way of life being re-created, a slice of modern social history is revealed.

Balmoral

★★ Queen Victoria's castle, still a royal retreat in the Highlands

7 miles W of Ballater; private house, open part year

Queen Victoria's attachment to the Highlands was profound. She and Albert first visited in 1842 and were instantly entranced. In 1848 they took a lease on 'a pretty little castle in the old Scottish style' set on the banks of the River Dee. Four years later they acquired the freehold, along with a brace of neighbouring estates, and set to work creating their own private, summer-time domain, surrounded by wild scenery and loyal tenants. The old house was demolished and replaced with a mansion more suited to their needs, and the landscape was remodelled with bridges, roads, monuments, cottages and farms.

After Albert's death in 1861, the Queen far preferred Balmoral to the gloom of Windsor and spent ever longer at her 'dear paradise'. Her presence made the Highlands fashionable and Balmoral spawned a rash of Baronial 'castles' from Perthshire to Caithness. The place is still a happy refuge for the Royal Family and the present Queen spends at least two months there every year. Prior to her arrival, the grounds and gardens are open to the public, along with the ballroom of the house itself.

Architecturally, Balmoral's only truly interesting feature is a colossal baronial tower, capped with turrets. Otherwise it could be mistaken for a minor public school. The architect was William Smith, and the interior is said to be cleverly designed for the needs of a large, complex household. Visitors see none of this, for the ballroom has its own separate entrance. This huge room has a Gothic-style ceiling and stags heads on the walls. A mirrored alcove to one side provides seating for royalty and favoured guests. Some of Queen Victoria's wedding gifts are on display, including a set of silver clansmen playing Highland Games. Paintings are of greater interest, including several Landseers and *The Stag Brought Home* by Carl Haag, that depicts a torch-lit scene outside the house. It is a wildly romantic image that reflects Victoria's own vision of her Highland home.

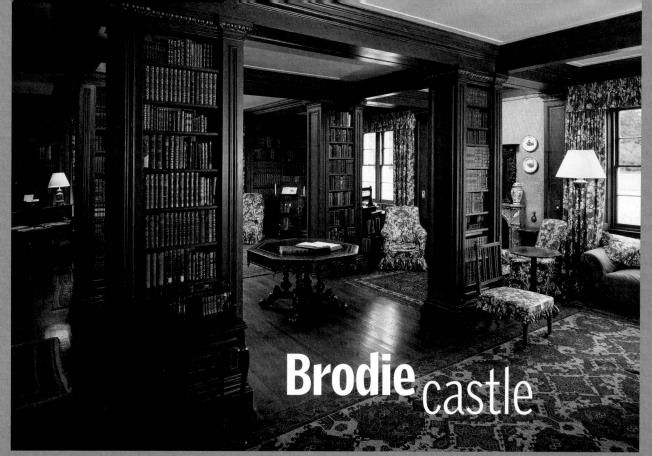

Brodie castle

Above The current library at Brodie Castle dates from the early Victorian refurbishment. It was created in 1846 out of two former storerooms by architect James Wylson for William, the 22nd laird of Brodie.

★★★ An historic house with fine 17th-century additions

4 miles W of Forres; National Trust for Scotland, open part year

The Brodies are an ancient family, claiming descent from Brude, king of the northern Picts in the 6th century. While this may be somewhat fanciful, they have certainly held lands in Moray since the 12th century. A carved stone on the present house bears the date 1567, suggesting that the builder was one Alexander Brodie, the 12th laird, a wild figure in his day, who was outlawed at one time for feuding with his neighbours. His new house, perhaps added to an older structure, followed the Z-plan then fashionable for towers, having a central block containing the hall and main apartments, with off-set towers placed diagonally at either end.

'Most charming of all is the
Blue Sitting Room, with ... robust,
naive plasterwork.'

Above The entrance hall – once the original kitchen of the castle – was designed by James Wylson in the 1840s. The low vaulted ceiling is supported by squat, Romanesque-style pillars. **Left** The plasterwork in the Blue Sitting Room bears the initials of the 15th laird and his wife Elizabeth Innes and probably dates from the brief years between their marriage, in 1635, and her death in 1640. It survived, therefore, the sacking of the castle by Royalist troops in 1645.

The 15th laird, also Alexander, is of particular interest. Married at just 17 and widowed five years later, he devoted the rest of his life to architecture and religious struggle. He had signed the National Covenant in 1638, a public petition that asserted the rights of Scots to worship God in a Church independent of the King, and served in Scotland's Parliament during the Civil War. His house was wrecked by Royalists in 1645, but afterwards he rebuilt the castle, which included a dining room with an extraordinary ceiling. It is something of a mystery as to why a Calvinistic laird should have commissioned such a voluptuous piece of plasterwork. The baroque ceilings at Holyrood and Thirlestane come close in their flamboyance, but even these stop short of showing bare-breasted maidens, fondled by wood nymphs. The ceiling must date from before Alexander's death in 1680, since his son was as penniless as he was pious: a fine of £4,800 levied against his father as a penalty for his Covenanting sympathies almost bankrupted the estate.

Later generations of Brodies continued to invest their all in the house. The 19th laird replaced the staircase and left this world with debts of more than £18,000. In the 1820s, William Burn enlarged the house for the 22nd laird, who was forced to sell the contents to settle the bill. A timely marriage to an heiress allowed him to create the wonderful library, its ceiling supported by the bookshelves. Most charming of all is the Blue Sitting Room, with another extraordinary ceiling where the robust, naive plasterwork is in complete contrast to the sophistication on view in the dining-room.

Cairness house

★★★ An unusual Georgian house laden with neo-classical symbolism

Near Cairness, 4 miles SE of Fraserburgh; private house, open part year

Cairness House dates from the late 18th century, when science and magic were equally in vogue. The house reflects both, combining rational design with a symbolism that speaks of secrets known only to adepts. In France, the mystical architect Claude Ledoux was experimenting with similar ideas, as were, to some extent, the English neo-classicists such as Soane and Dance. But there is no other country house in Britain that can rival the hermetic wonders designed into Cairness by James Playfair, the underrated father of the more celebrated William. A pair of broken columns artfully positioned by the portico are cut from standing stones plundered from a nearby 'Druid's Temple'. Set back from the severely neo-classical main block, side wings feature lunette niches framing sacrificial altars. The court that these wings enclose forms a perfect hemisphere approached through a tunnel arch that is astonishingly modern in its form. At the centre of the courtyard stands a circular ice-house, masquerading as a temple: the sinister, cavernous ice-pit within its windowless interior seems to echo with hidden meaning.

The house was built for Charles Gordon, heir to a Jamaican sugar fortune, on a plan that is rigidly symmetrical, even down to matching staircases. Downstairs in the main reception rooms, neo-classicism is taken to extremes, with full-length windows screened by columns – Ionic in the drawing room, Doric in the dining room – to create the effect of temple porticos. The oddest room of

Above The restored library is decorated in a Greek style. Major-General Thomas Gordon, the 2nd laird, was a great admirer of all things Greek and even fought in that country's War of Independence (1821–29).

all is the former billiard room, on the central axis off the entrance hall. Under a coved ceiling copied from Nero's baths at Baia, a frieze of hieroglyphs runs around the walls, with similar designs around the door, an unusual example of Georgian Egyptian style. On the first floor a top-lit corridor runs the full width of the house – an innovative concept for the time.

The Gordons sold the house in 1937 and after the Second World War it fell increasingly into decline. The present owners began their ambitious scheme of restoration and repair in 2001. Renovation work is still in progress, but the main rooms have already been decorated to spectacular effect. The neo-classical furniture now on display is in keeping with the house, and there are some fine pictures, including works by Raeburn, Cotes, Lely and Etty. Lying well off the beaten track, Cairness House is hard to find and harder still to understand, but it is worthy of the quest.

Castle **Fraser**

 A medieval castle, much remodelled over the centuries

16 miles W of Aberdeen; National Trust for Scotland, open part year

Although undeniably impressive, with romantic towers and exuberant architectural details, Castle Fraser has suffered from too much, rather than too little, attention over the years. The oldest part of the castle may already have existed when the Frasers were granted the estate by James II in 1454. By the 1570s they were well-connected lairds and Michael Fraser began to remodel the older building along more fashionable lines. The hall was extended and substantial towers – one square, one round – were added to opposing corners. Early in the 17th century, Michael's son Andrew added upper storeys similar to those at Craigievar (see page 168) and Crathes (page 173).

With the completion of the courtyard wings in the 1630s the exterior of the castle acquired its present form, but sadly the same cannot be said of the interior. The rooms were revamped in the 1790s and again in 1830s, when even the Great Hall did not escape unscathed. Later, the castle fell into decline, with leaking roofs and peeling walls, until it was bought by the hugely wealthy Viscount Cowdray in 1921. The Cowdrays spent a fortune restoring the castle to something like its former state, but it ceased to be a home after the Second World War.

The castle has now been restored still further by the National Trust for Scotland, and is in great demand for weddings and corporate events. Despite the building's rather lifeless character, there are intriguing features to be seen, including an enigmatic chamber hollowed from a wall under the laird's bedroom. Various uses have been proposed for the room – a 'laird's lug' for eavesdropping on conversations in the Great Hall, a safe deposit for valuable papers, or even, bizarrely, a prison cell. Another curious stone-vaulted room, said to have been a chapel, has a pair of hinged floorboards that may once have been the entry to a secret passage. The passage has been blocked by later work, but it remains a route through all the well-intentioned presentation into the castle's real past.

Corgarff castle

★ A remote military outpost with a violent past

Near Corgarff, 8 miles W of Strathdon; Historic Scotland, open part year

A lonely landmark on the bleak moors above the River Don, Corgarff has seen more than its share of trouble. It was built by the Forbes family in the mid-16th century, a plain and simple tower house in a remote location, and its isolation has made it vulnerable. In 1571 Margaret Forbes and 27 members of her family and household were burned to death when they refused to surrender to a raid by the Gordons. It was seized by Highland cattle-thieves in 1607, it was burnt again in the uprising of 1689, then it was used as a depot by retreating Jacobites in 1746. Two years later it was converted to a military outpost, housing a small garrison who were charged with the unenviable task of policing this notoriously lawless region and rooting out any lingering Jacobite insurgents. In the 1820s the army returned, this time to suppress the illicit whisky trade, but thereafter Corgarff fell into decay. It was last inhabited, by a pair of redoubtable old ladies, in 1914.

The castle has now been restored in its military guise, surrounded by a star-shaped wall designed to protect it from surprise attack. A barrack-room has been re-created on the first floor; up to sixteen men once slept, cooked and whiled away their tours of duty in a cramped and cheerless space such as this. To a trooper from the lowlands, the surrounding moors must have seemed as frightening and alien as the mountains of Afghanistan.

Craigievar castle

★★★★ The ideal Scottish castle of towers, turrets and enchantment

15 miles N of Banchory; National Trust for Scotland, open part year

Craigievar is one of Scotland's best-loved castles, combining fairy-tale architecture with a character of warmth and charm. In contrast to the cold splendour of many great historic houses, Craigievar appears enchantingly attractive as a home.

The castle's creator was William Forbes, the younger son of an old Aberdeenshire family, born in 1566. His elder brother Patrick was a leading churchman who inherited the family estate. William became a merchant and eventually made a fortune trading salted fish for timber through the Baltic ports, earning himself the nickname 'Danzig Willie'. In early middle age he married Margaret Woodward, daughter of an Edinburgh Lord Provost, and invested his money in land, accumulating a portfolio of bankrupted estates between Fife and Aberdeen.

Craigievar was acquired in 1610, right next to his brother's seat at Corse, where William had been raised. There was already a half-completed tower-house on the site, abandoned by the former owners. For reasons that may be readily imagined William decided to create a castle that would put his brother's home to shame. He employed as his designer John Bel, a master-mason who was responsible for some of the most splendid castles in northeast Scotland, including Fyvie (see page 181), Craigston (page 172), Castle Fraser (page 166) and Crathes (page 173). Bel excelled himself at Craigievar. He used the unfinished tower as a rugged plinth for a wildly romantic superstructure, which sits on an overhanging corbel-course high above the ground. There are some classical details, such as the balustrades around the viewing platforms on the roof, but there is no attempt at symmetry or

Below Lady Sempill's room is named after Lady Cecilia, wife of the 10th Lord Forbes and 19th Lord Sempill. She was responsible for refurbishing Craigievar in the 1940s; in many rooms, including her own bedroom, she had the dark wood panelling painted white. The portraits on either side of the bed are of Sir John Forbes and his wife Charlotte, who inherited the castle in 1823. They set about renovating and preserving Craigievar on the recommendation of their architect, John Smith.

'Forbes's descendants ... were beguiled by its antiquity ...'

Right Many of the bedrooms at Craigievar were once fitted with box-beds, most of which were removed in the 19th century. In the housekeeper's room, or ante room, one box-bed remains, albeit converted into a box-bath. **Far right** The Great Hall is spanned by a vaulted plasterwork ceiling bearing the date 1626. Stucco caryatids on the chimneypiece display the royal arms. The room was converted into a dining room by John Smith in 1825. He also enlarged and lowered the windows to allow better views of the surrounding landscape. Lady Cecilia Sempill's main alteration in the Great Hall was to introduce the Forbes tartan carpet and upholstery.

regulated order. What matters is the tower's solid mass, a statement of stability and strength, soaring skyward to support a little palace in the sky. A thrilling silhouette of turrets, roofs and chimneystacks stands out against the clouds.

There is an impressive hall and no fewer than eighteen apartments slotted into the six storeys, all linked with winding turnpike stairs. This is a building that looks back to a semi-mythic past, when lairds were noble warlords, yet it still provides elegant, comfortable accommodation suited to a Renaissance merchant-prince. Later architects took inspiration from such castles for the style known as Scots Baronial, but unlike the imitators, Craigievar was genuinely poised between the feudal and modern worlds. The ground-floor iron grilles and gun-ports could, if needs must, be put to real use.

The interior lives up to all expectations. Although William Forbes's descendants have made a number of alterations during their 350 years as lairds, they have never tried to change the antique character of Craigievar. If anything, they were beguiled by its antiquity and when staying at the castle

lived consciously anachronistic lives. In the mid-19th century the floors were still strewn with fresh
rushes every morning, as they had been since the castle was first built. Plumbing remained primitive;
in one small upstairs chamber a bath has been shoe-horned into a closet that once housed a box-bed.
Electricity still has not arrived, apart from a single socket installed for the cleaners.

The Great Hall is exceptional – indeed, although of fairly modest size, it is one of the finest rooms
in Scotland. The groin-vaulted ceiling is elaborately plastered, beautifully carved oak panelling lines
the walls, and the table and chairs have probably remained in constant use since the time of William
Forbes. Even the original screens passage is there. A purist might quibble at the sash windows, dating
from the 1820s, but they flood the room with light. Craigievar is not a fossil from the past, but a
house that reflects the passing of time. The one sad note is that, since the last laird's death in 1965,
the family has gone. Although the National Trust for Scotland has reverentially preserved the castle's
character, it cries out to be a loved and lived-in home.

Craigston castle

✪ ✪ A Renaissance tower house with some intriguing carvings

14 miles SW of Fraserburgh; private house, open part year

John Urquhart must have been a fascinating man. On his death, aged 84, in 1631 he was described by his relation, Sir Thomas Urquhart, as renowned 'for his deep reach of natural wit and great dexterity in acquiring many lands and great possessions'. In other words, he was a scholar with a flair for making money. The younger son of a powerful family from Cromarty, John Urquhart acquired Craigston in 1597 and built the present house between 1604 and 1607. The house has similarities with Craigievar and Fyvie, suggesting the involvement of John Bel, the talented master-mason in the region at the time, but there is an eccentricity to Craigston that must derive from Urquhart's own ideas.

The best bit is the carved parapet that projects from the entrance front over a tall arch. Although binoculars are needed to appreciate the details, five grotesque figures gaze down from the heights. They include David and Goliath, a pair of battling armoured knights and a piper. Inside, set into doors and shutters on the tower's principal floor, are carved wooden panels illustrating the Worthies, the Virtues, the Evangelists and Scottish kings. Such elaborate work may have been the height of fashion in Scotland's wealthiest Renaissance homes. Now, they are extremely rare.

John Urquhart did not seem to pass on his business talents to his son, who went bankrupt forcing Craigston's sale. The side wings, believed to be designed by William Adam, were added in the 1730s by Patrick Duff, who required more space for the thirty-six children that he sired. Then, in 1739, William Urquhart, a descendant of John, bought back the old home and it has remained with the family ever since. It is a fascinating warren, with many rooms scarcely altered or even decorated since the 19th century. The top-floor library is particularly atmospheric. Dusty and dim, it smells evocatively of old leather bindings. There are also several secret chambers, in one of which Jacobite fugitives were reputedly concealed after Culloden.

Crathes castle

★ ★ ★ A romantic castle with fine Renaissance painted ceilings

3 miles E of Banchory; National Trust for Scotland, open all year

Although lacking the fairy-tale enchantment of nearby Craigievar, Crathes belongs to the same tradition of ornate, romantic tower houses that constitute Scotland's most distinctive contribution to European architecture. Like many of its neighbours, it was designed by a master-mason known from inscriptions as I. Bel, who provided dream castles for the fashion-conscious lairds of the area during the later years of the 16th century. As was commonly the case, the Renaissance Crathes was a remake of an older, cruder structure for a even more ancient local family.

The Burnetts, or Burnards as they were called originally, were Anglo-Saxon exiles who came to Scotland in the 12th century during the reign of David I. Two centuries later, they were rewarded for their support of Robert the Bruce in his struggle for the crown with the grant of an estate in the royal forest of Drum. Their stronghold for many generations was a small crannog – an artificial island fort – on the Loch of Leys. In the 16th century, a useful marriage brought connections with the wealthy Abbey of Arbroath just before the Reformation. With the abbey's confiscated lands safely in their care, they began the construction of Crathes Castle in 1553.

Their plain, sturdily defensive tower still remains pretty much intact as the lower storeys of the present structure. The later, upper levels, marked off by an undulating string-course, constitute an altogether different

Above In 1323 Robert the Bruce rewarded his follower Alexander Burnard with the role of Royal Forester of Drum. He presented him with the Horn of Leys, possibly as a badge of office for the position.

Above In the Room of the Nine Nobles, the beamed ceiling was painted in the 16th century, but later covered over with lathe and plaster. When this was removed in the 19th century, decoration depicting nine great heroes from history and the Old Testament were revealed. **Left** The ceiling in the Muse's room is painted with sixteen women representing the Nine Muses and Seven Virtues.

programme; a veritable riot of turrets and caphouses, corbelling and waterspouts, chimney-stacks and decorated dormers designed purely for exuberant display.

The most precious possession in the castle is the famous Horn of Leys, a boar's tusk hunting horn given to the family by the Bruce himself. It has pride of place above the fireplace in the impressively baronial high hall. This room has seen many changes, including an enormous window gained in the 1870s. Sadly, it also lost almost all of its painted plasterwork, which was stripped off in the 1920s, perhaps in the mistaken belief that it was Victorian fakery. Elsewhere, some superb painted timber ceilings have survived, colourfully incorporating Scots Renaissance iconography: the Nine Nobles, Nine Muses and Seven Cardinal Virtues. Equally impressive is the long gallery, running the full length of the top-floor of the tower. It has a ceiling made from broad oak planks – a costly rarity in Scotland at the time – that have been extravagantly cut 'on the quarter' to best display the grain.

The Burnetts steered a careful course through the troubles of the 17th century, managing to keep their heads on their shoulders and their estates intact. In the reign of Queen Anne, Sir Thomas added a new wing to house his twenty-one children and planted the gardens' famous yews. A further wing was added in the 1870s by the 11th Baronet, who had made a fortune in America from real estate and ranching. The 13th baronet redesigned the gardens and, on his death in 1953, left the castle to the National Trust for Scotland. The family moved out in 1966 after the Victorian wing in which they lived was destroyed by fire. In James Burnett's delicately chosen words, they had felt they were intruding on the privacy of visitors.

Delgatie castle

★ A lovingly restored tower house with eclectic decor

Near Turriff, 17 miles SW of Fraserburgh; private house, open all year

Delgatie Castle was long a stronghold of the Hays, a family who fought bravely for the losing side in every civil conflict from the Catholic revolt against James VI in 1594 to the Jacobite uprising of 1745. A monument to pride and doomed ideals, their home declined in tandem with their fortunes and was left almost derelict after serving as a military hospital in the Second World War. In 1947 it was bought by Captain Hay, who, assisted only by his wife, a handyman and a few friendly volunteers, devoted more than thirty years to its restoration. At times it may have seemed a hopeless cause, but the project proved successful. Since the Captain's death in 1997, the building has been run as the Clan Hay Centre, a beguiling, mildly eccentric visitor attraction that still feels like a home.

Claims that the castle dates from 1030 can safely be ignored, unless some early fragment lies embedded and hidden in its core. The tower is more likely from the 16th century and has since grown through the years with a splendid disregard for architectural coherence. Rooms range from Renaissance to Victorian, all linked by a turnpike stair, over 5-feet wide, that rises within the thickness of the wall. Two bedchambers feature painted ceilings. One, dating from 1597, when the Hays returned from exile in France, includes a colourful bestiary of real and imagined creatures. Another originally showed naked maidens clutching tulips but is now little more than scriptural quotations, the naughty bits having been painted over in the 19th century.

'... a house that reaches **back through time.**

★★★ Castle with a medieval royal fortress at its core

10 miles SW of Aberdeen; National Trust for Scotland, open part year

Below The drawing room at Drum Castle was originally the high hall of the Jacobean house. In the 18th century it became a dining room, and was then transformed into the drawing room in the 19th century. Anna Forbes, wife of the 20th laird, oversaw the Victorian improvements; her portrait, by John Graham Gilbert, hangs over the fireplace.

Drum castle

Drum is a house that reaches back through time. Its massive tower of rough-hewn granite dates from the 13th century and is the relic of a royal fortress, granted by Robert the Bruce to William de Irwin in 1323. Drum Castle remained the Irvines's home until the 24th laird died in 1975.

In the early days, the Irvines feuded with their neighbours and fought off Highland clans. Later, as Royalists, they suffered at the hands of Cromwell. In the 18th century, as Jacobites, they lost most of their lands. Throughout their history, as opportunities arose, they altered and improved the family home.

Sometime in the 16th century a wing was added to the tower. Then, in 1619, the 9th laird built a larger range that now forms the south front. The following two centuries saw little change, with the family genteel but poor, but through hard work and good marriages their fortunes eventually revived. In the 1840s, the 18th laird transformed the medieval laigh hall into a library. Some forty years later his grandson modernized the lay-out, creating a new entrance front, complete with Baronial battlements and towers. Despite the house being made up of so many parts, the interior is surprisingly coherent. This is largely thanks to the skills of David Bryce, the architect who was commissioned to convert the rambling, antiquated complex into a comfortable home. But credit must be shared. After Bryce's death in 1876, his nephew John took over and the 20th laird's artistic wife, Anna Forbes, also played a part in the interior design.

The neo-Jacobean woodwork in the drawing room is most attractive. With a scattering of Eastern rugs and comfy settees by the fire, some fine paintings (including a few Raeburns) and a grand piano, the room is made for lazy, rainy country-house weekends. The library, in contrast, is more formal and imposing with a high barrel vault decorated with heraldic shields.

The castle's most memorable room is kept as a last surprise. Behind the east range, an outside stair climbs to a doorway on the first floor of the keep. From here, within the thickness of the wall, a narrow turnpike stair snakes up to a upper floor. This was once the medieval high hall, the private preserve of the laird's family. Now it is a vast, seemingly forgotten chamber, with a cavernous fireplace and bare stone walls.

Duff house

★★☆ William Adam's Baroque masterpiece

At Banff, 18 miles W of Fraserburgh; museum, open all year

Duff House proved to be William Adam's swansong, the last big country house that he designed and arguably his finest. Yet the project produced a bitter row that came close to destroying Adam's reputation.

Adam's client was William Duff, Lord Braco, a canny local laird who had vastly increased his fortune through shrewd investments in property and land. There were problems between them from the start, with frequent changes to the brief and disputes over the budget. Within eighteen months of construction starting in 1735, Braco was reluctantly giving in to Adam on the need for an attic storey "because the want of it would spoill the Looks of such a Monstrous house". But it was the cost of the stonework for the entrance front that was the last straw. The pediment, pilasters, figurines and roof-top vases were hand-carved at Adam's stone-yard at South Queensferry: Braco discovered, to his horror, that the vases alone cost 20 guineas each. He reckoned that his architect was overcharging him by £1,000 a year – the salary of a Minister of State.

Once the roof was in place, Braco suspended further work and refused to pay any money that he owed. Adam faced years of litigation before he won the case and the house remained a shell when he died in 1748. So great was Braco's fury that whenever he drove past he had the blinds of his carriage drawn shut.

His son eventually resumed building work in 1754, but even then it was years before Duff House was a habitable home.

Above The dining room has been restored to its original grey, a perfect foil for the 18th-century portraits that hang there. The portrait of Elizabeth Cunyngham by Allan Ramsay is considered to be the finest in the house.

Despite all the difficulties, the house is the most original and exciting that Adam ever built. It is very Scottish, with a soaring verticality that is emphasized by the absence of pavilion wings. The temple front, with giant Corinthian pilasters and elaborate heraldic carving on the tympanum, is a *tour de force* designed to honour Braco's name. No English Whig would have approved of such Baroque extravagance, but a Scottish laird liked his lineage to be properly displayed.

The interior, completed long after Adam's death, is fitted out in accordance with his plans. The reception rooms ascend in grandeur to the upper floors, culminating in a Great Drawing Room that forms a 30-foot cube, pushing up into the roof. Each bedroom suite is self-contained, with a little turnpike stair leading up to rooms for servants on a mezzanine floor.

The house is now in immaculate condition, but its recent history has been as fraught as the building's beginning. By the early 1900s the Duffs had acquired a dukedom through a royal marriage and were living at Mar Lodge, near Balmoral. This vertiginous ascent of the social summits had precipitated them into dire financial straits. In 1906, to save on the upkeep of Duff House, the Duke gave it to the town of Banff, much as a maharajah might give some luckless neighbour a white elephant. It was variously a hotel and a sanatorium before serving as a camp for German naval prisoners in World War II, when a Victorian wing was hit by a stray *Luftwaffe* bomb. Even when taken into state care in 1956 the house continued to languish, empty and ignored.

In 1992 the National Galleries of Scotland initiated an imaginative plan for the rebirth of Duff House. They provided works of art from their reserve collection and sourced appropriate furnishings, while Historic Scotland restored the fabric and decor of the house. The end result cannot be faulted. The grand reception rooms gleam with gold leaf. Superb paintings, including a magnificent El Greco, hang on the walls. Adam's masterpiece has at long last been accorded the respect that it deserves.

Dunnottar castle

★ ★ The dramatic ruins of a palatial cliff-top fortress

2 miles E of Stonehaven; private house, open all year

Set on a remote peninsular, with the waves pounding the rocky shore below, Dunnottar is thrilling to behold. The site was once almost certainly the Pictish centre of Dun Fothar and later housed a Celtic monastery. During the Wars of Independence, struggles for possession of the headland saw successive fortresses besieged, rebuilt and destroyed again.

Dunnottar was once home to the Keiths, a family honoured with the hereditary position of Earl Marischal. The seemingly impregnable position ensured that historic events were played out within and around the castle's walls. But by 1722, with the last Earl Marischal a penniless Jacobite exile, the contents were auctioned off and the buildings stripped to roofless shells.

The approach is dramatic, up a steep, well-guarded route, facing batteries of gun-loops. The broad, open plateau at the top is wind-blown and scattered with assorted ruins. The oldest of these is a late 14th-century tower house, with the remains of a smithy and stable-block beyond. Two free-standing lodgings, one above the curtain wall and another on the plateau, were built in the 16th century, probably by the hugely wealthy 4th Earl, known as 'William o' the Tower' because he spent his long and largely solitary life in this inhospitable location.

At the end of the 16th century, William's scholarly and well-travelled son, George, began building a Renaissance palace, the ruins of which perch on the cliff edge. It must have been stupendous in its heyday. The remains of halls, private chambers, a chapel and guest lodgings are ranged around what would have been a garden. One room was re-roofed and restored in the 1920s, but in a bland, unconvincing style. The basement level is the best preserved, with a labyrinth of passages and chambers, including a dark, dank vault that was used to imprison a large group of Covenanters in 1685.

Fyvie castle

★★☆ Edwardian opulence within a Renaissance building

Near Fyvie, 21 miles W of Peterhead; National Trust for Scotland, open part year

Since Fyvie ceased to be a royal stronghold in 1380, five families have sought to make it their dynastic base: the Prestons, Meldrums, Setons, Gordons and Leiths. Supposedly, each added a tower to the castle – Fyvie's five towers still bear their names – before the family declined, losing influence, wealth and finally their home. The castle, in contrast, grew from strength to strength.

Little remains of the castle of the Prestons and Meldrums, despite their namesake towers. By the time Sir Alexander Seton acquired Fyvie from Andrew Meldrum in 1596, it was a sprawling mansion built around a courtyard. Seton was a rising star who became Chancellor of Scotland after James VI's accession to the English throne. He was also something of a Rennaisance Man with a passion for architecture, and he transformed Fyvie into one of the greatest houses of the age, combining French sophistication with traditional Scottish forms. His south front is majestically imposing, with a soaring triumphal arch flanked by sturdy drum towers and a roof-scape of matching

'The castle ... grew from **strength to strength.**'

Above left The Great Stair is a wheel staircase, with steps some 10-feet wide. It is lit by 18th-century Venetian gondola lamps. **Above right** A portrait of Marie Louise January, the American wife of Lord Leith, hangs over the fireplace in the dining room. The French glass on the table was bought to celebrate the Leiths' golden wedding anniversary in 1921.

turrets. It is one of Scotland's first examples of symmetrical design, an early, somewhat casual, nod to classical ideals. Seton was also responsible for the castle's magnificent wheel staircase.

In 1694 the last of the Setons died in Paris, a Jacobite exile. In 1733, Fyvie was bought by William Gordon, the 2nd Earl of Aberdeen. At the time Gordon was also building Haddo House, just a few miles to the east. His second wife had already given him an heir to that estate, but a new marriage to a third wife meant he had another dynasty to house. Later in the century, his son William tore down older ranges at Fyvie and added a new wing, now known as the Gordon Tower.

The next great change in the castle's fortunes came in 1889 when, as a result of the spendthrift ineptitude of the last Gordon laird, the castle was sold to Alexander Leith, later Lord Leith. The multi-millionaire had made his fortune in the United States, but he was born just seven miles from Fyvie and had heard tales of his mother's ancestor, Sir Henry Preston. At the age of 42, Leith bought Fyvie and all its contents for £175,000 and thus reclaimed his Scottish roots. He modernized the house, installing plumbing, electricity and telephones, and acquired a picture collection that included fifteen Raeburns. Continuing the old tradition, he added a new tower. On its second floor, he created an ornately decorated gallery, designed by John Bryce as a *fin-de-siecle* take on Baronial dreams. With Brussels tapestries on panelled walls, a self-playing organ, a French Renaissance fireplace (genuine) and medieval portraits (fake), it adds up to an Aberdeenshire Xanadu.

In 1982 Alexander's great-grandson, Sir Andrew Forbes-Leith, put Fyvie and its contents up for auction. With the help of public funding, the National Trust for Scotland bought the castle and the palatial building has now been reinstated as it was a hundred years ago, in Alexander Leith's Edwardian heyday. Despite this latest change in ownership, there are no plans to add another tower.

Haddo house

★ ★ Robert Adam revival style in a William Adam house

17 miles SW of Peterhead; National Trust for Scotland, open part year

Haddo House holds up a mirror to the vagaries of upper-class good taste through the 18th and 19th centuries. The original design, by William Adam, was a strict interpretation of Palladian ideals for William Gordon, 2nd Earl of Aberdeen. Much to Adam's irritation, the Earl, who was noted for his meanness, employed a cheaper rival, John Baxter, to build the house. It was completed in 1735, but there have been many changes since, both in architecture and in decor, obliterating almost every element of Adam's finely tuned plan. The last major remodelling of the house was in the 1880s by the 7th Earl, later the 1st Marquess, and his wife Ishbel, a strong-willed, long-lived couple

Below Little remains of the William Adam's original decor at Haddo although some details have survived in the panelling of the entrance hall. The fireplace is a Victorian construction, made up of reclaimed pieces of medieval carving.

'... nothing is actually quite what it seems.'

Above The library at Haddo was given a deeply coffered, Adam-style ceiling during the 19th-century refurbishment. The bookshelves and panelling are of cedar wood, inlaid with ebony.

who dubbed themselves, rather archly, 'We Twa'. In their grand reception rooms, the ceilings, fireplaces and furniture form an impressively complete ensemble that could all be by Robert Adam. But nothing is actually quite what it seems. Haddo House represents one the earliest examples of Adam Revival style, with reproduction furniture and 'plasterwork' in papier mâché. The entrance hall, by contrast, is Baronial, featuring polished oak and painted panels. The library – panelled in cedar and hung with velvet curtains and pendulous brass chandeliers – is an oasis of Victorian masculinity. There is also an intriguing secret closet; perhaps the 7th Earl owned certain books he did not wish his devoted wife to find.

Throughout the house, portraits and mementoes record the family's contrasting careers. The 3rd Earl was a Georgian rake, who, despite being married to a pretty cook who had seduced him with her mutton chops, also kept mistresses in at least three other houses that he owned. His grandson, the 4th Earl, was Queen Victoria's Prime Minister from 1853 to 1855 and a pillar of respectability. The 6th Earl, who hated the responsibilities that came with his title, fled incognito to America where he worked as a seaman before vanishing off the coast of Nova Scotia in a storm. More recent Earls and Marquesses have led less colourful lives. The 4th Marquess left Haddo to the National Trust for Scotland on his death in 1974, although the family still retains an apartment in the house.

Leith hall

A comfortable country house with an interesting family history

7 miles S of Huntly; National Trust for Scotland, open part year

Although of no great architectural distinction, Leith Hall is intriguing, for it belonged to the same middle-class family for some 300 years before being given to the National Trust for Scotland in 1945. Given the lack of grandeur or glamour, the Trust has excelled in its presentation. The building's architectural development, from modest tower house to mansion, is charted alongside the history of the owners. The furniture and decor, paintings, photographs and personal possessions on display all play their part in a saga spanning nine generations.

The house is built around a central court, with each wing from a different period. The oldest, to the north, was built in 1649 by James Leith, whose merchant father had purchased the estate to give his family a 'landed' status. Times were hard, with civil war and famine, and Leith's descendants would face other vicissitudes. Several were Jacobites, one was murdered, another was a spendthrift fool, but there were also heroes, military and moral, along with some admirable heroines. James Leith's great-grandson modernized the house, creating the east wing from a former service range in 1756. A generation later, his son built the south wing in a homely version of Palladian design. Finally, the west side of the courtyard was closed off in 1868 when the 7th laird, 'Colonel Sebastian', added a Baronial range which included that most essential Victorian amenity – a billiard room.

The story ended sadly in 1939, when the 21-year-old 9th laird was killed in a motorcycle accident within months of inheriting the estate. At a time when many country houses were being abandoned or destroyed, his mother decided that Leith Hall should be offered to the Trust, which has ever since preserved both the building and the memories it holds.

Glossary

The aim in this book has been to avoid terms not familiar to the lay person. However, some specialist terms in common use in architectural circles may have crept in, for which the following may be helpful.

acanthus – pattern of an exotic Mediterranean flower with large leaves used in classical decoration.

anthemion – a honeysuckle flower pattern used in classical decoration.

Artisan Mannerist – buildings created by masons using pattern books (rather than architects) in the period c.1615–75. Mannerism originated in 16th-century Italy and was characterised by Classical elements used in unusual ways. It was taken up in the Low Countries, then spread to England.

ashlar – block of masonry fashioned into a wall, either load-bearing or to cover brick.

bailey, inner and outer – a fortified enclosure, usually moated and surrounded by a curtain wall, containing a motte (mound) with a keep on top. Walls are topped by battlements, with crenellations which protected defenders from arrows, and machicolations, or floor openings, through which attackers could be fired down on.

baluster – upright post supporting the handrail on stairs.

bargeboard – wooden board protecting the eaves of a roof.

bay – a space of wall between any vertical element, such as an upright beam, pillar or a division into a window or door.

bay window – window projecting out from a flat wall, either canted if the sides are straight, or bowed if curved.

bolection mould – moulding concealing the join of vertical and horizontal surfaces, shaped like an S in cross-section.

Boulle – elaborate inlay work on the surface of furniture, customary in 17th and 18th-century French work.

bow – see bay window

broch – see box, page 11

canted – see bay window

cartouche – frame for a picture or statue, often oval and surrounded by a scroll.

caryatid – a column in the shape of a draped female figure.

casements – see sashes

castle of enclosure – a form of early medieval castle in which individual buildings are enclosed within a curtain wall, in contrast to later medieval castles that consisted of a tower with subsidiary buildings in a courtyard to front or rear.

chinoiserie – a style of Rococo with Chinese motifs, often linked with Gothick.

coffering – a ceiling composed of beams enclosing sunken square or round panels.

collars – see roof timbers

corbel – a stone or wood projection in a wall that supports a beam, statue or sill.

cornice – (1) a ledge or projecting upper part of a classical entablature. (2) Moulding at the top of a wall concealing the join with the ceiling.

cottage ornée – late-Georgian/Victorian picturesque cottage, usually with thatched roof and Gothic windows.

crenellation – see bailey

crocket – Gothic decorative device, usually a cusp or curling leaf, at regular intervals on outer edges of spires, pinnacles and gables

cruck – a simple structure of two, usually curved, trunks of wood formed into an inverted V which support the walls and roof of a medieval house.

curtain wall – in castle-building, a wall constructed between defensive projections such as bastions.

dentil – one of a series of small square blocks along the base of a cornice

dorter – a sleeping room or dormitory, especially in a college or monastery.

dressing – a general term for finishings; stone is dressed to either a smooth or ornamental surface.

enfilade – a line of rooms in sequence along one side of a house, usually with interconnecting doors.

entablature – a feature of classical architecture comprising everything above column height, formally composed of architrave, frieze and cornice.

flatwork – decorative plaster or woodwork in low relief.

frontispiece – a decorative bay above a doorway in a Tudor or Jacobean building, customarily composed of Renaissance motifs.

gable – the triangular end of a double-pitched roof, sometimes with stepped or scrolled (Dutch) sides.

garderobe – privy or lavatory, usually discharging into a ditch or moat outside a medieval house.

Great Chamber – see solar

grisaille – monochrome painting, usually a mural and in shades of grey.

grotesque – decorative wall motif of human figures, as found in Roman grottoes.

half-timbering – term for timber-framed house derived from the practice of splitting logs in half to provide beams.

harling – rough-cast render, containing gravel.

hipped roof – a roof with a sloping end instead of an end gable.

Ho-Ho bird – chinoiserie motif associated with 18th-century Rococo style.

jetty or jettied floor – upper floor extended, or oversailed, beyond the lower one to give more space upstairs and protect lower walls from adverse weather. Jettying also uses the downward thrust of the upper walls to form a cantilever, preventing internal ceiling beams from bowing.

keep – see bailey

king post – see roof timbers

linenfold – a pattern on wall panels imitating folded linen.

louvre – a covered turret above a medieval hall that allowed smoke to escape.

machicolation – see bailey

mannerism – see Artisan Mannerist

mansard – a roof with two separate pitches of slope.

motte – see bailey

mullion – central divider of window, made of metal or stone.

oversail – see jetty

oriel – an upper window projecting from a wall, sometimes (incorrectly) used to indicate a tall medieval window lighting the dais end of the Great Hall.

Palladian – a style of classical architecture, formal and refined outside, often lavish inside, named after Italian architect, Andrea Palladio (1508–80). Moving spirit behind most English classical designers, especially Inigo Jones and, later, Lord Burlington, William Kent and the early Georgians.

parlour – see solar

piano nobile – the main ceremonial floor of a classical building, sitting on the basement or 'rustic' lower floor.

pier-glass – a wall mirror supported by a small table, bracket or console.

pietra dura – literally 'hard stone'; a decorative inlay using highly polished stones such as marble, jasper and porphyry

pilaster – a flat column projecting only slightly from a wall.

pointing – mortar or cement used to seal between bricks.

porte-cochère – a grand porch with a driveway through it, allowing passengers to alight from carriages under cover.

prodigy house – a large, ostentatious house of the Elizabethan/Jacobean period.

putti – unwinged sculptures of chubby boys found in Classical and Baroque decoration.

queen post – see roof timbers

quoins – dressed corner stones.

render – a covering of stucco, cement or limewash on the outside of a building.

Rococo – the final phase of Baroque style in the 18th century, typified by refined painted and plaster decoration, often asymmetrical and with figures.

roof timbers – a tie-beam runs horizontally across the roof space; a king post rises vertically from the tie beam to the apex of the roof; queen posts rise not to the apex but to subsidiary beams known as collars; wind-braces strengthen the roof rafters.

rustic – a name given in Palladian architecture to the lower floor or basement, beneath the piano nobile.

rustication – treatment of ashlar by deep-cutting joints so they look stronger or cruder.

sashes – windows opening by rising on sash ropes or cords, as opposed to casements which open on side hinges.

scagliola – composition of artificial stone that imitates appearance of grained marble.

Scots Baronial – see box, page 13

screens passage – accessed from the main door of a medieval building and built into one end of a Great Hall to shield it from draughts. Doors or arches lead from the passage into the hall on one side and kitchens on other. Above is usually a minstrels' gallery.

Serlian – motifs derived from pattern books of the Italian Renaissance architect, Sebastiano Serlio (1475–1554).

sgraffito – plaster decoration scratched to reveal another colour beneath.

solar – the upstairs room at the family end of a medieval hall, originally above an undercroft or parlour. Originally accessed by ladder or spiral stairs, it was usually replaced by a Great Chamber in the Tudor era.

strapwork – strap or ribbon-like decorative scrolls in Elizabethan and Jacobean design.

stucco – plaster, usually protective, covering for brick, sometimes fashioned to look like stone.

studding – vertical timbers laid close to each other to strengthen the wall. Close-studding tends to indicate wealth.

tie-beam – see roof timbers

tower house – compact, fortified house arranged vertically, with rooms over several storeys; the main chamber, or hall, is usually on an upper floor with a vaulted room below. Tower houses were a popular form in Scotland and still built up until the 17th century.

undercroft – a vaulted room or crypt beneath a building, partly or wholly underground

vault – a ceiling, usually of stone composed of arches.

Venetian window – Palladian window composed of three components, the centre one arched.

wind-braces – see roof timbers

Contact details

Note: Readers are advised to check opening times before visiting, either via the websites and addresses below or in Hudson's Historic Houses & Gardens, the annual guide to castles, houses and heritage sites open to the public.

Aberdeen: Provost Skene's House – Guestrow, off Broad Street, Aberdeen, AB10 1AS www.aagm.co.uk Tel 01224 641086 Open all year, daily 10am–5pm (1–4pm on Sun)

Alloa Tower – Alloa Park, Alloa, Central, FK10 1PP www.nts.org.uk Tel 0844 493 2129 Open late Mar–late Oct, daily 1–5pm

Arniston House – Gorebridge, Midlothian, EH23 4RY www.arniston-house.co.uk Tel 01875 830515 Open early Apr–mid-Sep, Tue & Wed (also Sun, Jul–mid-Sep) for tours at 2pm & 3.30pm

Arnol Blackhouse – Arnol, Isle of Lewis, HS2 9DB www.historic-scotland. gov.uk Tel 01851 710395 Open all year, Mon–Sat 9.30–5.30 (to 4.30pm, Oct–Mar)

Ballindalloch Castle – Ballindalloch, Banffshire, AB37 9AX www.ballindallochcastle.co.uk Tel 01807 500205 Open Good Fri–late Sep, Sun–Fri 10.30am–5pm

Balmoral Castle – Balmoral, Ballater, Aberdeenshire, AB35 5TB www.balmoralcastle.com Tel 01339 742534 Open Apr–Jul, daily 10am–5pm; also open Nov–mid-Dec, Wed 11am–2pm for guided tours

Blackness Castle – Blackness, West Lothian, EH49 7NH www.historic-scotland.gov.uk Tel 01506 834807 Open all year, daily 9.30am–6.30pm (to 4.30pm, Oct–Mar)

Blair Castle – Blair Atholl, Pitlochry, Perthshire PH18 5TL www.blair-castle.co.uk Tel 01796 481207 Open all year, daily (Tue & Sat in late Oct–late Mar) 9.30am–4.30pm

Blairquhan – Straiton, Maybole, Ayrshire, KA19 7LZ www.blairquhan.co.uk Tel 01655 770239 Open mid-Jul–mid-Aug, Tue–Sun 2–4.45pm, at other times by appointment

Borthwick Castle Hotel – Borthwick, North Middleton, Midlothian, EH23 4QY www.borthwickcastle.com Tel 01875 820514

Brodick Castle – Isle of Arran, KA27 8HY www.nts.org.uk Tel 0844 493 2152 Open late Mar–late Oct, daily 11–4.30pm (to 3.30pm in Oct); park open daily, all year, 9.30am–dusk

Brodie Castle – Forres, Moray, IV36 2TE www.nts.org.uk Tel 0844 493 2156 Open late Mar–late Oct, daily (Sun–Thur, May–Jun & Sep–Oct) 10.30am–5pm; grounds open all year, daily

Burn's Cottage – Alloway, Ayrshire, KA7 4PY Tel 01292 441215 Open all year, daily 10am–5.30pm (to 5pm, Oct–Mar)

Cairness House – Lonmay, Fraserburgh, Aberdeenshire, AB43 8XP www.cairnesshouse.com Tel 01346 582078 Open early Apr–late Sep, Mon, Wed, Fri & Sun 10am–4pm, for tours on the hour

Callendar House – Falkirk, FK1 1YR www.falkirk.gov.uk Tel 01324 503770 Open all year, Mon–Sat 10am–5pm (and on Sun 2–4pm, Apr–Sep)

Castle Campbell – Dollar, Central, FK14 7PP Tel 01259 742408 Open all year, daily (Sat–Wed, Oct–Mar) 9.30am–5.30pm (to 4.30pm, Oct–Mar)

Castle Fraser – Sauchen, Inverurie, Aberdeenshire, AB51 7LD www.nts.org.uk Tel 0844 493 2164 Open late Mar–late Oct, Wed–Sun & BH Mon (daily in Jul–Aug) 11am–5pm (from 12pm in Oct); grounds open all year, daily

Castle Menzies – Weem, Aberfeldy, Perthshire PH15 2JD www.menzies.org Tel 01887 820982 Open early Apr–mid-Oct, daily 10.30am–5pm (from 2pm Sun)

Castle of Mey – Thurso, Caithness, KW14 8XH www.castleofmey.org.uk Tel 01847 851473 Open early May–late Sep, daily 10.30am–4pm (closed for two weeks, late Jul/early Aug)

Cawdor Castle – Nairn, Morayshire, IV12 5RD www.cawdorcastle.com Tel 01667 404401 Open early May–mid-Oct, daily 10am–5pm

Corgarff Castle – Strathdon, Aberdeenshire, AB36 8YP www.historic-scotland.gov.uk Tel 01975 651460 Open all year, daily (Sat–Sun, Oct–Mar) 9.30am–6.30pm (to 4.30pm, Oct–Mar)

Craigievar Castle – Alford, Aberdeenshire, AB33 8JF www.nts.org.uk Tel 0844 493 2174 Open late Mar–late Aug, Fri–Tue (daily in Jul–Aug), 12–5.30pm for guided tours only; grounds open all year, daily

Craigston Castle – Turiff, Aberdeenshire, AB53 5PX Tel 01888 551228/551640 Open during various weeks in the summer; contact for further information

Crathes Castle – Banchory, Aberdeenshire, AB31 5QJ www.nts.org.uk Tel 0844 493 2166 Open all year, daily (Wed–Sun, Nov–Mar) 10.30am–5.30pm (to 4.30pm in Oct, to 3.45pm in Nov–Mar); gardens open all year, daily 9am–dusk

Crichton Castle – Pathhead, Midlothian, EH37 5QH www.historic-scotland.gov.uk Tel 01875 320017 Open Apr–Sep, daily 9.30am–6.30pm

Culross Palace – Culross, Fife, KY12 8JH www.nts.org.uk Tel 0844 493 2189 Open late Mar–late Oct, Thur–Mon (daily, Jun–Aug) 12–5pm (to 4pm, Oct)

Culzean Castle – Maybole, Ayrshire, KA19 8LE www.nts.org.uk Tel 0844 493 2149 Open late Mar–Oct, daily 10.30am–5pm

Dalmeny House – South Queensferry, West Lothian, EH30 9TQ www.dalmeny.co.uk Tel 0131 331 1888 Open Jul–Aug, Sun–Tue 2–5.30pm

Dean Castle – Dean Road, Kilmarnock, East Ayrshire, KA3 1XB www.deancastle.com Tel 01563 522702/578155 Open all year, Wed–Sun 11am–5pm for guided tours only

Delgatie Castle – Triff, Aberdeenshire, AB53 5TD www.delgatiecastle.com Tel 01888 563479 Open all year, daily 10am–5pm

Dirleton Castle – Dirleton, East Lothian, EH39 5ER www.historic-scotland.gov.uk Tel 01620 850330 Open all year, daily 9.30am–6.30pm (to 4.30pm, Oct–Mar)

Doune Castle – Doune, Central, FK16 6EA www.historic-scotland.gov.uk Tel 01786 841742 Open all year, daily (Sat–Wed, Oct–Mar) 9.30am–5.30pm (to 4.30pm, Oct–Mar)

Drum Castle – Drumoak, by Banchory, Aberdeenshire, AB31 5EY www.nts.org.uk Tel 0844 493 2161 Open late Mar–late Oct, Sat–Mon, Wed–Thur & Fri on a BH weekend (daily in Jul–Aug) 12.30–5pm (from 11am, Jul–Aug); grounds open all year, daily

Duart Castle – Isle of Mull, PA64 6AP www.duartcastle.com Tel 01680 812309/01577 830311 Open Apr–early Oct, daily (Sun–Thur in Apr) 10.30am–5.30pm (11am–4pm in Apr)

Duff House – Banff, Aberdeenshire, AB45 3SX www.duffhouse.org.uk Tel 01261 818181 Open all year, daily (Thur–Sun, Nov–Mar) 11am–5pm (to 4pm, Nov–Mar)

Dumfries House – due to open to the public in summer 2008; check the offficial website (www.dumfries-house.org.uk) for updated information

Dun Carloway – Carloway, Isle of Lewis, HS2 9DY Tel 01851 643338 Open all year, daily 10am–5pm

Dunnottar Castle – Stonehaven, Kincardineshire, AB39 2TL www.dunechtestates.co.uk Tel 01569 762173 Open all year (weather permitting), daily 9am–6pm, Easter to Oct (2–5pm on Sun), 10.30am to dusk, Nov to Easter

Dunrobin Castle – Golspie, Sutherland, KW10 6SF www.highlandescape.com Tel 01408 633177 Open early Apr–mid-Oct, daily 10.30am–4.30pm (to 5.30pm, Jun–Sep; opens 12pm on Sun, Apr–Jun and Sep-Oct)

Dunvegan Castle – Dunvegan, Isle of Skye, IV55 8WF www.dunvegancastle.com Tel 01470 521206 Open all year, daily 10am–5.30pm (11am–4pm, Nov–mid-Mar)

Edinburgh: Craigmillar Castle – Craigmillar Castle Road, Edinburgh, EH16 4SY www.historic-scotland.gov.uk Tel 0131 661 4445 Open all year, daily 9.30am–6.30pm (to 4.30pm, Oct–Mar)

Edinburgh: Edinburgh Castle – Castlehill, Edinburgh, EH1 2NG www.edinburghcastle.gov.uk or www.historic-scotland.gov.uk Tel 0131 225 9846 Open all year, daily 9.30am–6pm (to 5pm, Oct–Mar)

Edinburgh: The Georgian House – 7 Charlotte Square, Edinburgh, EH2 4DR www.nts.org.uk Tel 0844 493 2108 Open daily, Mar–Nov (11am–3pm in Mar & Nov; 10am–5pm, Apr–Jun & Sep; 10am–7pm, Jul–Aug)

Edinburgh: Gladstone's Land – 477b Lawnmarket, Edinburgh, EH1 2NT www.nts.org.uk Tel 0844 493 2120 Open late Mar–late Oct, daily 10am–5pm (to 7pm in Jul–Aug)

Edinburgh: Holyrood Palace – Canongate, The Royal Mile, Edinburgh, EH8 8DX www.royalcollection.org.uk Tel 0131 556 5100 Open all year, daily 9.30am–6pm (to 4.30pm in Nov–Mar). Opening arrangements may be subject to change at short notice

Edinburgh: John Knox House – 43–45 High Street, Edinburgh, EH1 1SR Tel 0131 556 9579 Open all year, Mon–Sat (daily in Jul–Aug) 10am–5pm (12–4pm on Sun & to 7pm on Mon–Sat in Aug)

Edinburgh: Lauriston Castle – 2a Cramond Road South, Davidson's Mains, Edinburgh, EH4 5QD www.cac.org.uk Tel 0131 336 2060 Open all year, Sat–Thur (Sat–Sun in Nov–Mar) for guided tours at 11am, 12pm, 2pm, 3pm & 4pm (at 12pm, 2pm & 3pm in Nov–Mar); grounds open daily, 9am–dusk

Edinburgh: Mary King's Close –2 Warriston's Close, Writers Court, Edinburgh, EH1 1PG www.realmarykingsclose.com Tel 0870 243 0160 Open all year, daily 10am–9pm (to 4pm on Sun–Fri, Nov–Mar) for pre-booked tours

Edzell Castle – Edzell, Angus, DD9 7UE www.historic-scotland.gov.uk Tel 01356 648631 Open all year, daily 9.30am–6.30pm (to 4.30pm, Oct–Mar)

Eilean Donan Castle – Dornie, Kyle of Lochalsh, Wester Ross, IV40 8DX www.eileandonancastle.com Tel 01599 555202 Open mid-Mar–mid-Nov, daily 10am–6pm

Falkland Palace – Falkland, Cupar, Fife, KY15 7BU www.nts.org.uk Tel 0844 493 2186 Open early Mar–late Oct, daily 10am–5pm (from 1pm on Sun)

Fort George – Ardersier, by Inverness, IV1 2TD www.historic-scotland.gov.uk Tel 01667 460232 Open all year, daily 9.30am–6.30pm (to 4.30pm, Oct–Mar)

Fyvie Castle – Turriff, Aberdeenshire, AB53 8JS www.nts.org.uk Tel 0844 493 2182 Open late Mar–late Oct, Sat–Wed (daily in Jul–Aug) 12–5pm (from 11am, Jul–Aug); garden open all year, daily

Glamis Castle – Glamis, by Forfar, Angus, DD8 1RJ www.glamis-castle.co.uk Tel 01307 840393 Open Mar–Dec, daily 10am–6pm (11am–5pm, Nov–Dec)

Glasgow: Holmwood House – 61–63 Netherlee Road, Glasgow, G44 3YG www.nts.org.uk Tel 0844 493 2204 Open late Mar–Oct, Thur–Mon 12–5pm

Glasgow: Pollok House – 2060 Pollokshaws Road, Glasgow, G43 1AT www.glasgowmuseums.com & www.nts.org.uk Tel 0141 616 6410 & 0844 493 2202 Open all year, daily 10am–5pm; park open daily, all year

Glasgow: The Tenement House – 145 Buccleuch Street, Glasgow, G3 6QN www.nts.org.uk Tel 0844 493 2197 Open Mar–Oct, daily 1–5pm

Gosford House – Longniddry, East Lothian, EH32 0PX Tel 01875 870201 Open mid-Jun–mid-Aug, Fri–Sun 2–5pm

Greywalls Hotel – Muirfield, Gullane, East Lothian, EH31 2EG www.greywalls.co.uk Tel 01620 842144

Haddo House – Ellon, Aberdeenshire, AB41 7EQ www.nts.org.uk Tel 0844 493 2179 Open late Mar–early Nov, Fri–Mon (daily in Jul–Aug) 11am–5pm for guided tours only; grounds open all year, daily

The Hill House – Upper Colquhoun Street, Helensburgh, Dunbartonshire, G84 9AJ www.nts.org.uk Tel 0844 493 2208 Open late Mar–late Oct, daily 1.30–5.30pm

Hill of Tarvit – Cupar, Fife, KY15 5PB www.nts.org.uk Tel 0844 493 2185 Open late Mar–late Oct, Thur–Mon (daily in Jun–Aug) 1–5pm (to 4pm in Oct); estate open all year

Hopetoun House – South Queensferry, West Lothian, EH30 9SL www.hopetounhouse.com Tel 0131 331 2451 Open early Apr–late Sep, daily 10.30am–4pm

The House of Dun – Montrose, Angus, DD10 9LQ www.nts.org.uk Tel 01674 810264 Open late Mar–late Oct, Wed–Sun & BH Mon (daily in Jun–Aug) 12.30–5.30pm (from 11.30am in Jun–Aug) for guided tours only; gardens open all year, daily 9am–dusk

House of the Binns – Linlithgow, West Lothian, EH49 7NA www.nts.org.uk Tel 0844 493 2127 Open Jun–Sep, Sat–Wed 2–5pm; grounds open daily, all year

Hugh Miller's Cottage – Church Street, Cromarty, Inverness, IV11 8XA www.nts.org.uk Tel 0844 493 2158 Open late Mar–late Sep, daily (Sun–Wed in Oct) 12.30–4.30pm

Inchcolm Abbey – Inchcolm, Fife www.historic-scotland.gov.uk Tel 01383 823332 Open Apr–Sep, daily 9.30am–6.30pm. Castle is reached by ferry, ring 0131 331 5000 for information

Inveraray Castle – Inveraray, Argyll, PA32 8XE www.inveraray-castle.com Tel 01499 302203 Open Apr–Oct, daily 10am–5.45pm (from 12pm on Sun)

Inveraray Jail – Church Square, Inveraray, Argyll, PA32 8TX www.inverarayjail.co.uk Open all year, daily 9.30am–6pm (10am–5pm, Nov–Mar)

Jarlshof – Sumburgh Head, Shetland, ZE3 9JN www.historic-scotland.gov.uk Open Apr–Sep, Mon–Sun 9.30am–5.30pm

Kelburn Castle – Fairlie, By Largs, Ayrshire, KA29 0BE www.kelburncountrycentre.com Tel 01475 568595 Open Jul–Aug for guided tours by arrangement

Kellie Castle – Pittenweem, Fife, KY10 2RF www.nts.org.uk Tel 0844 493 2184 Open late Mar–late Oct, daily 1–5pm; gardens open all year, daily 9.30am–5.30pm

Kinloch Castle – Isle of Rum, PH43 4RR Tel 01687 42037 Open Mar–Oct, Mon–Sat for tours by arrangement

Kisimul Castle – Castlebay, Isle of Barra, HS9 5UZ www.historic-scotland.gov.uk Tel 01871 810310 Open Apr–Sep, Mon–Sun 9.30am–5.30pm

Leith Hall – Huntly, Aberdeenshire, AB54 4NQ www.nts.org.uk Tel 0844 493 2175 Open Easter, then May–Sep, Sat–Sun (& Fri & Mon on a BH Weekend, daily in Jul–Sep) 12–5pm; grounds open all year, daily

Lennoxlove House – Haddington, East Lothian, EH41 4NZ www.lennoxlove.com Tel 01620 823720 Open Jul–Oct, Tue, Thur & Sun 3–5pm

Linlithgow Palace – Linlithgow, West Lothian, EH49 7AL www.historic-scotland.gov.uk Tel 01506 842896 Open all year, daily 9.30am–6.30pm (to 4.30pm, Oct–Mar)

Lochleven Castle – Loch Leven, Kinross, KY13 8U www.historic-scotland.gov.uk Tel 07778 040483 in summer, 07767 651566 at other times Open Apr–Oct, daily (Sat–Wed in Oct) 9.30am–5.30pm (to 4.30pm in Oct). Reached by ferry from Kinross, last ferry departs one hour before closing time

Mount Stuart – Isle of Bute, PA20 9LR www.mountstuart.com Tel 01700 503877 Open Easter, then May–Sep, Sat–Fri 11am–5pm, (10am–2pm on Sat); garden open daily 10am–6pm

New Lanark – New Lanark Mills, Lanark, South Lanarkshire, ML11 9DB www.newlanark.org Tel 01555 661345 Open all year, daily 10.30am–5pm (from 11am, Sep–May)

Newark Castle – Port Glasgow, Strathclyde, PA14 5NH www.historic-scotland.gov.uk Tel 01475 741858 Open Apr–Sep, daily 9.30am–6.30pm

Newhailes – Newhailes Road, Musselburgh, East Lothian, EH21 6RY www.nts.org.uk Tel 0844 493 2125 Open Easter, then May–Sep, Thur–Mon 12–5pm for tours (reservations 0131 653 5599); estate open daily, all year

Orkney: Broch of Gurness – Aikerness, Orkney, KW17 2NH www.historic-scotland.gov.uk Tel 01856 751414 Open Apr–Sep, daily 9.30am–6.30pm

Orkney: Corrigall Farm – Harray, Orkney, KW17 2LQ www.orkney.org/museums Tel 01856 771411 Open Mar–Oct, daily 10.30am–1pm & 2–5pm (2–5pm on Sun)

Orkney: Earl's Palace – Watergate, Kirkwall, Orkney, KW15 1PD www.historic-scotland.gov.uk Tel 01856 875461 Open Apr–Sep, daily 9.30am–6.30pm

Orkney: Kirbuster Farm – Birsay, Orkney, KW17 2LS www.orkney.org/museums Tel 01856 771268 Open Mar–Oct, daily 10.30am–1pm & 2–5pm (2–5pm on Sun)

Orkney: Skaill House – Sandwick, Orkney, KW16 3LR www.skaillhouse.com Tel 01856 841501 Open Apr–Sep, daily 9.30am–6.30pm (a joint ticket is available with Skara Brae)

Orkney: Skara Brae – Sandwick, Orkney, KW16 3LR www.historic-scotland.gov.uk Tel 01856 841815 Open all year, daily 9.30am–6.30pm (to 4.30pm, Oct–Mar)

Scone Palace – Perth, PH2 6BD www.scone-palace.co.uk Tel 01738 552300 Open Apr–Oct, daily 9.30am–5.30pm

Stirling: Argyll's Lodging – Castle Wynd, Stirling, FK8 1EJ www.historic-scotland.gov.uk Tel 01786 431319 Open all year, daily 9.30am–6pm (to 5pm, Oct–Mar)

Stirling Castle – Castle Wynd, Stirling, FK8 1EJ www.historic-scotland.gov.uk Tel 01786 450000 Open all year, daily 9.30am–6pm (to 5pm, Oct–Mar)

Stobhall – Stobhall, Cargill, Perthshire, PH2 6DR www.stobhall.com Tel 01821 640332 Open early Jun–early Jul, Tue–Sun, for tours at 2pm, 3pm & 4pm (library open by arrangement)

Torosay Castle – Craignure, Isle of Mull, PA65 6AY www.torosay.com Tel 01680 812421 Open Apr–Oct, daily 10.30am–5pm; gardens open all year, daily 9am–7pm

Urquhart Castle – Drumnadrochit, Loch Ness, IV63 6XJ www.historic-scotland.gov.uk Tel 01456 450551 Open all year, daily 9.30am–6.30pm (to 4.30pm, Oct–Mar)

Index

Main entries for houses are in **bold**

T=top TL=top left TR=top right B=bottom BL=bottom left BR=bottom right
L=left R=right C=centre CL=centre left CR=centre right

Front Cover Country Life/Simon Jauncey (corridor leading to the Tapestry Room, Dumfries House) **Back Cover** Courtesy of Duart Castle (Duart Castle) **Endpapers** Reproduced by kind permission of The National Trust for Scotland (Drawing Room wall stencils, The Hill House) **1** By kind permission of the Sutherland Trust (Wildcat from the Sutherland arms, Dunrobin Castle) **2-3** Collections/Colin Inch (Craigievar Castle) **4-7** European Map Graphics Ltd. **8** John Sinclair/johnphotographer@hotmail.com **11** © Reader's Digest/Illustration by Hardlines Ltd. **12** William Adam by Unknown (detail), Scottish National Portrait Gallery **13** © Reader's Digest/Illustration by Hardlines Ltd. **14-15** Collections/Ross Graham **16** Scottish Viewpoint/ Gary Doak **17** Scottish Viewpoint/Paul Tomkins/VisitScotland **18 TL** Scottish Viewpoint/Paul Tomkins/VisitScotland **R** Courtesy of Blair Castle **19** The Interior Archive/Christopher Simon Sykes **20** Reproduced with kind permission of Falkirk Council Cultural Services **21** Reproduced by kind permission of The National Trust for Scotland **22 L** Scottish Viewpoint/Doug Houghton **R** Reproduced by kind permission of The National Trust for Scotland **23-24** Reproduced by kind permission of The National Trust for Scotland **25** © Crown Copyright Reproduced Courtesy of Historic Scotland **26 CL** Collections/Archie Young **B** © Crown Copyright Reproduced Courtesy of Historic Scotland **27** Collections/Philip Craven **28-30** Courtesy of Glamis Castle **31-33** Reproduced by kind permission of The National Trust for Scotland **33 R** The Interior Archive/Christopher Simon Sykes **34 L** Scottish Viewpoint/Dennis Barnes **34-35** Reproduced by kind permission of The National Trust for Scotland **36** www.lastrefuge.co.uk/Adrian Warren **37** Scottish Viewpoint/Paul Tomkins/ VisitScotland **38-39** By kind permission of the Rt Hon Earl of Mansfield and Mansfield, Scone Palace, Perth **40** The Interior Archive/Christopher Simon Sykes **41** © Crown Copyright Reproduced Courtesy of Historic Scotland **42-43** Collections/Dennis Barnes **43** www.bridgeman.co.uk/ Scottish National Portrait Gallery, Edinburgh **44-45** © Crown Copyright Reproduced Courtesy of Historic Scotland **46-47** www.maxmilligan.com **48-49** www.britainonview.com/Chris Close **50-52** Country Life/Paul Barker **53** Scottish Viewpoint/John Pringle **54** Courtesy of Borthwick Castle Hotel **55** Scottish Viewpoint/Paul Tomkins/VisitScotland (inset) Scottish Viewpoint/John Pringle **56-57** Scottish Viewpoint/ VisitScotland **58** © Crown Copyright Reproduced Courtesy of Historic Scotland **59** Scottish Viewpoint/Paul Tomkins/VisitScotland **60-62** © Crown Copyright Reproduced Courtesy of Historic Scotland **63-64** Reproduced by kind permission of The National Trust for Scotland **64 B** Collections/Michael Jenner **65** Reproduced by kind permission of The National Trust for Scotland **66** www.britainonview.com **67-68** The Royal Collection © 2008 Her Majesty Queen Elizabeth II (photo: Peter Smith) **69** Scottish Viewpoint/Bob Lawson **70 T & B** The Interior Archive/Fritz von der Schulenburg **71** The Real Mary King's Close **72-73** The Interior Archive/Christopher Simon Sykes **74** Courtesy of Greywalls Hotel **75** www.britainonview.com **76-77** Collections/Michael Jenner **77** Scottish Viewpoint/ VisitScotland **78** Collections/ Michael Jenner **79** Collections/Archie Young **80** © Crown Copyright Reproduced Courtesy of Historic Scotland **81** tonymarshphotography.com **82** www.britainonview.com/Dennis Barnes **83** © Crown Copyright Reproduced Courtesy of Historic Scotland **84-85** Reproduced by kind permission of The National Trust for Scotland **86-87** David Lyons **88** The Interior Archive/ Fritz von der Schulenburg **89 T** www.britainonview.com **B** Collections/Frank Fitzpatrick **90-91** Reproduced by kind permission of The National Trust for Scotland **92** Andrew Scott-Martin **93-94** Country Life/Simon Jauncey **95-103** Reproduced by kind permission of The National Trust for Scotland **104** Courtesy of Kelburn Castle **105** Collections/Frank Fitzpatrick **107** New Lanark Conservation **108-109** www.britainonview.com/David Noton **110-111** © Crown Copyright Reproduced Courtesy of Historic Scotland **112-113** Reproduced by kind permission of The National Trust for Scotland **114** The Interior Archive/Christopher Simon Sykes **115** Courtesy of the Castle of Mey. **116-117** David Lyons **117** Scottish Viewpoint/Paul Tomkins/VisitScotland **118** Cawdor Castle Ltd **119** Courtesy of Duart Castle **120-121** www.britainonview.com/Derek Croucher **122** The Interior Archive/ Christopher Simon Sykes **123-124** By Kind Permission of the Sutherland Trust **125-126** David Lyons **127** Photograph supplied from the Dunvegan Castle library by kind permission of the 30th Chief of Clan MacLeod, Hugh MacLeod of MacLeod. **128-129** Scottish Viewpoint/Paul Tomkins/VisitScotland **129 T** David Win **130** Collections/ Archie Young **131** www.lastrefuge.co.uk/Adrian Warren **132** Reproduced by kind permission of The National Trust for Scotland **133** Collections/Ed Gabriel **134 L** The Interior Archive/ Christopher Simon Sykes **134-135** Nick McCann/Heritage House Group **135 R** Nick McCann/ Heritage House Group **136 L** www.britainonview.com/Dennis Barnes **R** Collections/Frank Fitzpatrick **137** Charles Tait **138** © Crown Copyright Reproduced Courtesy of Historic Scotland **139** Collections/Michael Jenner **140-141** The Interior Archive/Christopher Simon Sykes **142** Charles Tait **143-145** Keith Hunter Photography **146** The Interior Archive/ Christopher Simon Sykes **147** Charles Tait **148** Scottish Viewpoint/Paul Tomkins/VisitScotland **149-153** Charles Tait **154 L** Scottish Viewpoint/VisitScotland **154-155** Collections/Dennis Barnes **156-157** Reproduced by kind permission of The National Trust for Scotland **158** Courtesy of Aberdeen Art Gallery & Museums © Mike Davidson, Positive Image **159** Courtesy of Ballindalloch Castle **160** David Lyons **161-163** Reproduced by kind permission of The National Trust for Scotland **164-165** Courtesy of Cairness House **166** Reproduced by kind permission of The National Trust for Scotland **167** David Lyons **168-171** Reproduced by kind permission of The National Trust for Scotland **172** © David Lacy-Hulbert **173-174** Reproduced by kind permission of The National Trust for Scotland **175** Courtesy of Delgatie Castle **176-177** Reproduced by kind permission of The National Trust for Scotland **178** Collections/Archie Young **178-179** The Interior Archive/Christopher Simon Sykes **180** David Lyons **181-182** Reproduced by kind permission of The National Trust for Scotland **183 T** Collections/Dennis Barnes **B** Reproduced by kind permission of The National Trust for Scotland **184** The Interior Archive/Christopher Simon Sykes **185** Reproduced by kind permission of The National Trust for Scotland

Discover Britain's Historic Houses: Scotland

Writer Hamish Scott

Reader's Digest Project Team
Series editor Christine Noble
Art editor Jane McKenna
Picture researcher Christine Hinze
Caption writer/copy editor Caroline Smith
Proofreader Ron Pankhurst
Indexer Marie Lorimer
Product production manager Claudette Bramble
Production controller Katherine Bunn

Reader's Digest General Books
Editorial director Julian Browne
Art director Anne-Marie Bulat
Managing editor Nina Hathway
Picture resource manager Sarah Stewart-Richardson
Pre-press account manager Dean Russell

Colour origination Colour Systems Limited, London
Printed and bound in Europe by Arvato, Iberia

We are committed to both the quality of our products and the service we provide to our customers. We value your comments, so please feel free to contact us on **08705 113366** or via our web site at **www.readersdigest.co.uk**

If you have any comments or suggestions about the content of our books, you can contact us at: **gbeditorial@readersdigest.co.uk**

Published by The Reader's Digest Association Limited, 11 Westferry Circus, Canary Wharf, London E14 4HE

www.readersdigest.co.uk

This book is part of a series, *Discover Britain's Historic Houses*, designed and produced by Reader's Digest using material from *England's Thousand Best Houses*, written by Simon Jenkins and first published by Allen Lane, the Penguin Press, a publishing division of Penguin Books Ltd.

Concept code UK0149/L/S
Book code 634-0011 UP0000-1
ISBN 978 0 276 44386 2
Oracle code 356600011H.00.24